from
the
ashes…

from the ashes...

the future of the Conservative Party

Leading politicians and commentators speak out
Edited by Sam Gyimah

www.bowgroup.org

List of authors

David Cameron MP
Rt Hon Kenneth Clarke QC MP
Andrew Cooper
Rt Hon David Davis MP
Alan Duncan MP
Nick Gibb MP
Damian Green MP
Justine Greening MP
Michael Gove MP
Robert Halfon
Andrew Lansley CBE MP
Rt Hon Francis Maude MP
Rt Hon Theresa May MP
Archie Norman
Rt Hon Sir Malcolm Rifkind QC MP
Stephan Shakespeare
David Willetts MP
Tim Yeo MP

Acknowledgements

I am pleased the Bow Group is helping facilitate the debate on the future of the Conservative Party, which Michael Howard sensibly called for last May. For this, I am hugely grateful to the contributors to this volume, all of whom gave their time and words for free. All have contributed because they believe a Conservative Government will be good for Britain and that debating what the party stands for openly and candidly is a necessary step in achieving this.

Great thanks are owed to Intelligent Marketing and Methuen Publishing for working to my unrealistically tight deadlines; Malcolm Gooderham and Nigel Roberts for wise council; Camilla Barker for perseverance; Simon Baker and Anuj Goyal for inspiration and ideas; Kwasi Kwarteng for a free rein; Irene Harris for practical common sense; Katharine Roseveare for late nights typesetting and proof reading. Without the efforts of this team, none of this would have been possible. Finally, of course, thanks to my mother without whose single-handed and superhuman efforts I would not be where I am today.

Sam Gyimah
September 2005

Publishers

First published in Great Britain in 2005 by

Bow Publications Limited
1A Heath Hurst Road
London
NW3 2RU
www.bowgroup.org

Politico's Publishing, an imprint of
Methuen Politico's Publishing
11-12 Buckingham Gate,
London
SW1E 6LB
www.methuen.co.uk

© The Copyright for the individual contributions resides with the individual contributors.

A catalogue record for this book is available at the British Library.

ISBN 1-84275-151-4

Printed and bound in Sweden by Kristianstad Book Printers.

Designed and typeset by Intelligent Marketing www.intelligent-marketing.com.

All rights reserved. No part of this publication may be reproduced or transmitted in any form or by any means, electronic or mechanical including photocopying, recording or information storage or retrieval system without the prior permission in writing of the publishers.

CONTENTS

Introduction — 11

Conservatism - Public Service — 18
David Cameron MP

Time is Running Out — 28
Rt Hon Kenneth Clarke QC MP

What Does the Conservative Party Stand for? — 34
Andrew Cooper

Power to the People — 44
Rt Hon David Davis MP

Get Real or Die — 52
Alan Duncan MP

There is Such a Thing as Society — 56
Damian Green MP

Talking About a Revolution — 62
Nick Gibb MP

It's Foreign Policy, Stupid — 70
Michael Gove MP

A Winning Formula — 78
Justine Greening MP

A Just Society — 84
Robert Halfon

Power of Positive Politics — 92
Andrew Lansley CBE MP

Reassembling the Jigsaw — 102
Rt Hon Theresa May MP

Values for a New Century — 110
Rt Hon Francis Maude MP

The Problem is Us — 122
Archie Norman

Back to the Future — 130
Rt Hon Sir Malcolm Rifkind QC MP

No Easy Way Out — 138
Stephan Shakespeare

A 20/20 Vision for Britain — 142
David Willetts MP

Decline and Fall — 148
Tim Yeo MP

About the editor

Sam Gyimah

Sam Gyimah co-founded and is co-Managing Director of Clearstone Ltd, a company which trains the unemployed and low – paid as Heavy Goods Vehicle drivers and places them into jobs. Prior to starting his own business he was an investment banker at Goldman Sachs International. Sam is involved with a number of charities; he sits on the boards of Nacro Community Enterprises; was on the board of an inner London school for three years; and is on the Development Board of Somerville College, Oxford. He is Research Secretary of the Bow Group and a Ward Vice Chairman of the Hampstead and Highgate Conservative Association. He graduated from Somerville College, Oxford in 1999 with a degree in Philosophy, Politics and Economics and was President of the Oxford Union.

Introduction

What struck me as I watched the results tumble in on election night 2005 is that, for the Conservative Party, very little seems to have changed since 1997. It has been in a 'persistent vegetative state' for the last 8 years, and it seems to me that nothing short of a complete rebirth will halt its drift into electoral oblivion. But rebirth into what? And who should be in charge of the delivery? *From the ashes… the future of the Conservative Party* explores the views of leading politicians and commentators on how the Party could overcome the most dangerous challenge it has faced in 150 years.

It's a complicated problem, but what all of the contributors agree on is that it's all about *identity*. The Party needs to work out clearly and unambiguously the confusing issue of what it stands for in a way that speaks to ordinary people and grapples with their everyday problems.

> "The Party needs to work out clearly and unambiguously the confusing issue of what it stands for"

Collapse of the Conservative vote

All the contributors were asked to answer the same question from their own unique perspectives: what political agenda should the Conservative Party pursue to help secure victory at the next election? There was no collaboration between the contributors, and yet almost all agree that the last parliament "for all its tactical successes was a strategic failure"; as Andrew Lansley puts it: "in 1992, the Conservative Party polled 14 million votes" and in 2005, it polled 8.8 million votes. "For every vote gained direct from Labour, the Liberal Democrats gained two".

> "For every vote gained direct from Labour, the Liberal Democrats gained two"

Andrew Cooper brings his polling experience to bear in the most excoriating attack on the Party's record, pointing out that among under 35s, the age group among whom it did best in 1979, the Party came third. The Conservative vote fell in half the regions of England making the Party even more of a Southern rump. Support among ABC1s and women – historically the bedrock when the Party was winning – also fell significantly.

Nor can any comfort, Cooper argues, be taken from the number of seats won. Of the 31 seats gained from Labour, 18 were won not because of voters switching from Labour to the Conservatives but from Labour votes swinging to the Liberal Democrats. The results from the last three elections bear out Cooper's conclusions. Understanding why the Party's share of the vote has remained at a depressing 33% for the best part of 12 years and how to reverse the decline is more challenging.

> "Of the 31 seats gained from Labour, 18 were won not because of voters switching from Labour to the Conservatives but from Labour votes swinging to the Liberal Democrats"

The problem is the party itself

The problem according to Archie Norman is the Conservative Party itself. In a lucid and articulate contribution, he appears to agree with the Harvard psephologist Pippa Norris, who reflected on the Conservative Party's predicament in a seminal essay last year: "As in therapy, the first step towards recovery is to recognise a problem; the second is summoning a will to change". Conservatives, Norman points out have a cosy desire to believe that nothing is fundamentally wrong. "The orthodoxy after 1997 was that Tony Blair and new Labour, was not the real thing". The latter version of this delusion is that "they have failed to deliver and are wrecking the economy".

> "Conservatives have a cosy desire to believe that nothing is fundamentally wrong"

Cooper highlights the gulf between the Conservative Party and the rest of the country when he points out that of all the devastating evidence published in Michael Ashcroft's "wake up call to the Conservative Party", the most startling are the graphs showing that "Tory pronouncements which had the most positive impact on the enthusiasm of Conservative voters at the last election also had the most negative impact on floating voters".

Robert Halfon, who was the Conservative Parliamentary Candidate in Harlow, sums it up effectively when he points out the five negatives he came across on the doorsteps of a constituency that Winston Churchill and Norman Tebbit represented and, until 1997, returned a Conservative MP (Jerry Hayes), were:

1. The Conservatives do not stand for anything
2. The Conservatives do not reflect our aspirations
3. The Conservatives are opportunistic
4. The Conservatives are the party of 'toffs' and care little about the poor
5. The Conservatives speak in a language we don't understand.

No easy way out

Assuming the diagnosis of the Conservative problem is accurate there is still no easy solution. For example, the majority of the contributors appear to agree with Michael Portillo's comment that "if a party does not change, then voters are implicitly being required to say they were the ones who got it wrong". This contrasts sharply with the views of Conservative voters of whom eight out of ten think the Party is "on the right track" to get back into power before long, while barely a quarter of non-Tories think the same.

It has been argued that the party's values need to reflect more closely the values of the country but Stephan Shakespeare, in an interesting tack for a pollster, highlights the weaknesses of polling and rightly points out that the mission should precede the polling and not vice versa.

"the mission should precede the polling and not vice versa"

There is little consensus or clarity on what the Party should not be doing, never mind what it should be doing. Francis Maude is against 'aping' Tony Blair, or reaching for the treacherous terrain that is the Middle ground. Archie Norman argues you cannot "spray – paint new enthusiasms and new policies on an old chassis". Theresa May argues against simply completing the Thatcher revolution or a modernisation strategy that simply means "being less strident in tone, more caring or nicer younger gayer, than the Tories of the '80s'". To David Willetts, pledging to be more compassionate and forward – looking is not sufficient. It is worth noting that a number of the contributors lay claim to the tradition of One Nation Conservatism as the vision for the future. There are a number of consistent themes that run through the contributions in this book that could form the basis of a Conservative revival.

Trust is everything

Nick Gibb rightly argues that a conservative revival depends on winning back public trust. It has often been argued that the public are fed up with politics, but as Halfon points out, they are fed up with political parties and politicians and that is why the membership for political parties has fallen whilst that of pressure groups has risen. The implications of a lack of trust in the Conservative Party is summed up eloquently by Lansley when he

"we can have all the policies we like, even policies the public like, but if the public do not trust us, they will not endorse our policies"

argues "we can have all the policies we like, even policies the public like, but if the public do not trust us, they will not endorse our policies".

To win trust, Conservatives have to realise that conventional adversarial and tribal politics' which is often out of kilter with the reality, is a turn off for the electorate. Tactical opportunism like opposing the government when it is right or pursuing an agenda the party believes in (promoting choice in public services) only lowers the esteem of Conservatives in the eyes of voters.

MPs, as David Cameron lucidly argues, should behave in the House of Commons as they do in their constituencies – as proper public servants. Conservatives therefore have to deny themselves what Lansley refers to as the easy "attack dog options". In a similar vein, Norman calls for the test to be "what would we do if we were in government". And, instead of expending energy seeking to further lower Labour in the voter's eyes, Michael Gove argues, "we need to apply ourselves to elevating our position in the view of fellow citizens".

Compassionate Conservatism

The Conservative Party could elevate its position in the eyes of the voters by demonstrating that it cares for ordinary people. It seems the Left in Britain has monopolised the politics of compassion as Conservatives have too often sounded like the 'Economics Party', knowing the cost of everything but the value of nothing. Interestingly, Ken Clarke and Tim Yeo argue that a

"It seems the Left in Britain has monopolised the politics of compassion as Conservatives have too often sounded like the 'Economics Party', knowing the cost of everything but the value of nothing"

coherent critique and economic vision is central to revitalising the Party's fortunes. All the contributors appear to agree with Damian Green assertion that "anyone with a social conscience has found it a struggle to vote Conservative in the last few elections" and call for the party to vigorously and genuinely pursue a political agenda for the people and places politics has forgotten.

Empowering the individual

Central to all the contributions is the argument put forward by Alan Duncan that government does not necessarily have all the answers, a corollary of which is that more power and responsibility should be given to lower tiers of government if not the people. David Davis makes the general point that people will always make better decisions for themselves than government or any bureaucrat ever will. He drives the point home when he argues that freedom is essentially about empowerment and therefore central to creating an opportunity society.

> "freedom is essentially about empowerment and therefore central to creating an opportunity society"

Reforming public services

Choice and devolution in public services (health, education and policing) Davis passionately argues are vital to empowering individuals and ensuring that "state failure is not depriving people of opportunity and vulnerable people of their liberty". Public service reform proves to be a thorny issue for the contributors. The unanswered question at the heart of the contributions can be summed up as: "Do voters want a piece of mind or a piece of paper"?

The family

Another sensitive issue for the contributors is social policy, especially in support of the family, where there is an obvious tension between recognising that modern families come in different shapes and sizes and supporting marriage.

Cameron puts forcefully a point made by Davis, Lansley, Maude and Green amongst others; that a modern Conservative Party should stand up for marriage and use "the law, the tax and benefits system" to encourage families to get together and stay together, especially as "all the evidence suggests that children benefit most from having both parents – mother and father involved together in their upbringing".

Cameron and May go further than supporting the family as an institution, and call for policies that help families cope with the rigours of day - to - day life. May argues that a Ministry for the Family would cut across departments and show that Conservatives understand the needs of families caught in the trap of dealing both with childcare and caring for elderly relatives. Clarke however argues that lifestyle issues 'are very often about hard economics and income'.

Déjà vu?

If your response to this discussion is: "Haven't we heard it all before?" I am not surprised. In 1999, William Hague tried the Common Sense Revolution which was focussed on health and education. In 2002, Iain Duncan Smith made helping the vulnerable and social justice his key emphases. In 2003, Michael Howard kicked off his leadership at the Saatchi Gallery with a clear and positive statement of his beliefs.

Despite these attempts at a positive message, in every general election since 1997, it seems to me that Conservatives have ended up campaigning on narrow negative issues. In 1997, it was 'New Labour, New Danger'. In 2001 '10 days to save the Pound' became the memorable slogan and, in 2005, "reflexive blue collar whinges about Britain took the place of any positive argument for Conservative ideas".

What the contributions in *From the ashes...* highlight for me is the heartening fact that the necessary ideas for change do exist within the minds of today's leading Conservative thinkers. But history also warns that paying lip – service to the agenda for change is simply not an option. It seems to me that the only way the Party can persuade a cynical electorate that it has grasped the thorny nettle of change is to demonstrate this through its actions on a daily basis.

> "history also warns that paying lip service to the agenda for change is simply not an option."

I believe that pursuing an agenda for change has to be a one way street for the Party: there is no way back. Baroness Thatcher's time in office gives us a very pertinent example of how to pursue a change agenda. To halt the decline into which the country was sliding, she had to have a clear and non-negotiable agenda for change. Changing the country meant taking tough decisions and facing down vested interests. And, whilst opinions on the success of her premiership vary wildly, no one can deny that the agenda for change was pursued relentlessly with vigour and passion.

Incidentally, Tony Blair's approach to changing his Party is the same as Thatcher's approach to changing the country. Not surprisingly new Labour changed beyond recognition after Blair, and so did the country after Thatcher.

In fact you will not find a definitive answer to the question of identity. So what does *From the ashes...* offer? At one level it offers a wide - ranging reflection on a debate that has so far been limited to Westminster and think tanks in London, and yet will determine how our democracy functions for decades to come.

At another level it highlights powerfully that the Conservative Party has to be reborn into a party whose very DNA exudes trust, competence, compassion, real answers; and, above all, an inspiring vision and ideal for the country. The Party cannot wait for the political pendulum to swing back, it has to realise that "it has the power within itself to make the world" again.

The Conservative Party makes its most important contribution when it argues for the changes that are needed to make our country great. The Conservative Party is and will always be passionately concerned not just with individuals but with society. The instinctive Conservative approach of backing wealth creation, cutting regulation and keeping taxes low is just the start

David Cameron MP
Shadow Secretary of State for Education & Skills

David Cameron was born in 1966 and is the Member of Parliament for Witney. Educated at Eton and Oxford, David is a rising star of the Party, having only entered Parliament in 2001. He rose to prominence as Head of Policy Coordination under Michael Howard, having been blooded as a Special Adviser to Norman Lamont during the ERM crisis.

Prior to becoming an MP, David was the Head of Corporate Affairs at Carlton Communications Plc. He is married to Samantha, a successful creative designer and artist and has one son. David is a passionate advocate for special needs education.

Public Service

One thing that works very well in politics is the relationship between an MP and their constituents. There's an important lesson in this.

We behave completely differently in our constituencies to the way we behave at Westminster. At Westminster, we're constantly trying to gain the upper hand. We take every opportunity to do our opponents down. We're too often obsessed with the *process* of politics, rather than the *outcome* we want to achieve.

In our constituencies, we're proper public servants. MPs, whatever their party, work for their constituents, whatever their party affiliation. We're calm and reasonable. We don't score points; we help solve people's problems. We try to understand what's going wrong, and how it can be put right. We bring people together to tackle issues. And we look at them from a long-term perspective. These are some of the reasons why I love being a constituency MP.

We shouldn't forget these things when we walk through the doors of the House of Commons. We're not there to play partisan games. We're there to make a contribution to a better society. Politics is about public service. It's about working with people to help deliver the things they value and desire.

> "Politics is about public service. It's about working with people to help deliver the things they value and desire"

Politics with a purpose

We want a dynamic economy that generates the wealth to deliver rising living standards and better public services.

We want a decent society that gives people the freedom to live the lives they want, but which supports families and cares for the vulnerable.

We want to be part of a strong, self-confident and outward-looking country, a country we can be proud of.

On the centre right of politics, we have a distinctive idea about how to achieve these things. We recognise that government doesn't have all the answers, and we instinctively assume the best in people. We trust people. We don't see people as a problem to be *handled* by government. We see people who have problems needing to be *helped* by government. We don't view society from above, like some national project to be managed, directed and monitored. We look at society from the bottom up. Individuals. Families. Communities. Voluntary organisations and faith groups. Businesses. All the complex wonder of a modern, diverse country.

We do think there's such a thing as society, we just don't think it's the same thing as the state.

And we do believe in our country. We believe that Britain has a particular place in the world. Our place is to be a force for good, standing up for liberty, prosperity and the rule of law. These ideals are inextricably linked in our world-view. I think that Britain needs these Conservative insights, beliefs and approaches today.

> "We do think there is such a thing as society, we just don't think it's the same as the state"

In the era of globalization, we'll never achieve our economic potential if we smother our economy with excessive taxation and regulation – the instinctive approach of the left. In these more open and less deferential times, we'll never achieve a decent society with top-down government initiatives – the instinctive approach of the left. And in an increasingly unpredictable world, we'll never be the strong, self-confident country we can be if we treat the nation state as out of date – again, the left's instinctive approach.

Our agenda is more appealing to today's Britain than the Left's – if we can ensure that the country sees it for what it is, rather than what the Left says it is. Our goals – a dynamic economy, a decent society, a strong self-confident nation – are forward-looking, inclusive, and generous. We should never allow our opponents to caricature us as the opposite of these things. And we should remember that you never get anywhere by trashing your own brand.

> "In the era of globalization, we'll never achieve our economic potential if we smother our economy with excessive taxation and regulation"

The Conservative Party makes its most important contribution when it argues for the changes that are needed to make our country great. The Conservative Party is and will always be passionately concerned not just with individuals but with society. Conservatives believe profoundly that there is a 'we' in politics as well as a 'me.' The Conservative Party has always stood for and will always stand for aspiration and compassion in equal measure. If we don't make these things clear, it will be as if half the members of a finely-tuned orchestra just stand up and walk off the stage. The audience will hear too much brass and not enough strings.

I am a Conservative. I'm also a moderniser. I don't see any contradiction between these two statements.

The modernisation agenda

To be relevant in the modern world, we need to respect diversity in society. We need to have more women in leading roles. We need to be less confrontational. We need to be more informal and personal.

But I don't regard any of that as modernisation. It's just common sense.

Real modernisation goes deeper. Real modernisation is about your approach to politics. It means three things.

The first is to stick to your beliefs and principles even when – in fact especially when – there's a temptation to score a political point. We should never allow ourselves to create an impression of insincerity and inconsistency by attacking the Government when it does the right things. Real modernisation means agreeing with the Government when it does the right things.

"We need to respect diversity in society. We need to have more women in leading roles. We need to be less confrontational"

An example from a debate I'm involved is the Government's City Academy programme. There's a huge coalition building up to oppose the Government on Academies. Labour backbenchers. The teaching unions. Many LEAs. Large parts of the educational establishment. Influential press commentators. It's incredibly tempting for an opposition to score points by opposing Academies.

But I've been to the Peckham Academy and the Harris City Technology College in Croydon, and I simply ask myself these questions: is it right to get businesses involved in funding education? Is it right to direct resources to inner city areas where children from disadvantaged backgrounds have had a poor start in life? Is it right to give schools freedom to innovate and specialise?

My answer to all these questions is a resounding 'yes.' And that's why I won't oppose the Government on Academies. I will back them, and make as many constructive proposals as I can to improve them.

This relates to an argument you hear quite a lot in the Conservative Party these days. Some Conservatives say that what we need is 'clear blue water' between ourselves and Labour.

I think that's crazy. I came into politics to do the right thing and make a difference. I didn't come into politics to engage in some positioning exercise. Imagine if the doctrine of 'clear blue water' applied in the commercial world. You're a supermarket chain up against Tesco, who's offering 'good food at low prices.' I know: we'll offer 'bad food at high prices.' It's no different in politics.

The second thing I mean by real modernisation is thinking for the long-term. We need to carry out a clear and uncompromising assessment of the scale and nature of the fundamental challenges facing modern Britain. And then we should be honest about what that means. We should never simply tell people what they want to hear. You can only lead change if you're prepared to tell people uncomfortable truths in the interests of progress.

And third, real modernisation means evaluating ideas and policies on the basis of how they would actually work in practice.

This means there are three tests we need to apply to every idea and policy we develop during this Parliament.

- Is it true to our fundamental beliefs and principles?
- Is it in the long-term interests of the country?
- And will it work?

Creating a dynamic economy

The first thing our Party must get right is our stance on finance. We need an honest appraisal of economic realities.

Britain is in a strong position relative to many other European countries. But a modern politics means understanding that there are serious challenges. China is producing two million graduates a year. India is opening more than 1,300 engineering colleges. Eastern Europe is attracting more inward investment. Our savings ratio has fallen dramatically. The costs of transport congestion are rising. Our productivity is lower than the average for the G7. We've fallen down the international competitiveness league.

In the face of these challenges, the instinctive Conservative approach of backing wealth creation, cutting regulation and keeping taxes low is just the start. Real modernisation means developing our human capital by transforming vocational training and expanding higher education. So we will have to say honestly how these things will be paid for. Real modernisation means getting our transport infrastructure right so we're equipped to

"The first thing our Party must get right is our stance on finance. We need an honest appraisal of economic realities"

operate efficiently in the 21st century. If that involves charging for roads, we should say so.

In other words, we need to make it clear that we have a shared responsibility for creating a dynamic economy.

Tackling social breakdown and its consequences

There is one institution that is massively undervalued in our society. It brings up children with the right values. It takes care of the elderly and the sick. It helps those who are left behind. It can make us happy when we're sad. That institution is the family.

But look what's happening in our society today. Six year olds are wandering the streets of some of our cities looking for a hot meal and an adult who will take them to school. Eleven year olds are beating each other up and filming it on their mobile phones. Fourteen year olds are getting pregnant. Children are having children.

> "We should use the law, the tax and benefits system and other mechanisms to encourage families to get together and stay together."

Modern families come in all shapes and sizes – and they all need support. But real modernisation means facing up to the facts. All the evidence shows that children benefit most from having both parents – mother and father – involved together in their upbringing. And the evidence also shows that married couples have a better chance of staying together longer.

So a modern Conservative party should support marriage.

We should use the law, the tax and benefits system and other mechanisms to encourage families to get together and stay together. And we have to stop Government from doing things that undermine the family.

But modernisation goes much further than that. Time is one of the greatest enemies of family life today. So business has a role. We need companies to provide creative solutions to childcare for their employees. Many leading companies already do – for example offering workplace crèches. Companies should adapt their working practices to allow families to spend more time together.

> "Real modernisation means having the confidence to say that there is more to life than money. If the pursuit of material wealth and personal advancement ends in damaged and broken families, then that's a price not worth paying"

Public Service

Understanding that we are all in this together, that we have a shared responsibility for these things, means something else. It means recognising that there's been an unmistakeable coarsening and vulgarising of national life in recent years, and modern politics should not allow this trend to go unchallenged.

What's the impact of highly sexualized music videos, magazines and TV programmes on issues like sexual health and teenage pregnancy? What's the impact of food marketing on children's behaviour? What's the impact of the legal industry in fostering the rights culture and a growing sense that nothing is an individual's responsibility any more? We all have a part to play in addressing these issues, not least private companies, since many of these cultural changes are driven by business.

And individuals, too, must take more responsibility. There is no more important job in our society than raising children – it's a responsible one. It should profoundly affect the way that people live their lives.

Real modernisation means having the confidence and the courage to say that there's more to life than money. If the pursuit of material wealth and personal advancement ends in damaged and broken families, then that's a price that's not worth paying. It's our responsibility as politicians to give a lead on these issues, because the cost of family breakdown is shared by all of us.

Reforming public services

If you work hard, you can buy a bigger car, move into a better house, take the family on a better holiday. But you have to rely on the same school and the same hospital. People are frustrated – particularly when they know so much extra money has gone into public services. What the last eight years shows is that if you don't have an incredibly clear idea about how you want to reform public services, you won't really get anywhere.

There could not be an area where it is more important to understand what shared responsibility means. Labour have completely confused the roles of the national government, local government, and the social sector. In

"What the last eight years shows is that if you don't have an incredibly clear idea about how you want to reform public services, you won't really get anywhere."

education, Labour have failed to provide rigour in exam standards – which is a duty of central government. But they've massively interfered in the running of every school – which is not their responsibility at all. In crime, they've failed to provide a framework of clear and tough sentences – which is a duty of government. But they micro-manage every police force with ridiculous targets – going way beyond the boundaries of their proper responsibility.

Conservatives should have three priorities for public services. First, we must roll up our sleeves and get stuck in to the nitty – gritty. That's what I've been doing in education. Focusing on how to improve our state schools. Literacy in primary schools. Standards and discipline in secondary schools. A commitment to excellence and rigour in every part of the system.

Second, we should where at all possible devolve power to the local level. There are two types of devolution : giving more power and responsibility to lower tiers of government, and giving more power and responsibility directly to people. I want the Conservative Party to champion both.

Policing is a prime candidate for the devolution treatment. Directly elected police commissioners would help make the police accountable to local people and their priorities. As part of a wider package of police reform, they would help deliver the type of active, beat – based policing that people desperately want.

But real modernisation means more than the devolution of power. The problems that blight our most deprived neighbourhoods are complex and interconnected. Unstable and chaotic home environments. Low expectations. Poor schooling. Generational unemployment. Drug abuse and welfare dependency. Poor quality architecture and design. These problems can never be tackled by government, national or local, acting on its own.

"Policing is a prime candidate for the devolution treatment. Directly elected police commissioners would help make the police accountable to local people and their priorities"

The third priority is to give more responsibility for social action to the people who very often have the best solutions. People like the thousands of creative, dynamic and above all effective social enterprises and voluntary organisations within our communities. Social entrepreneurs make an inspirational contribution to our communities. We need to give them more power, to do more good.

But the social sector will only be a full partner for social action when the public sector learns how to let go. When it says to the youth club teaching kids excluded from school, the drug rehab with the best record of helping people straighten out their lives, or the faith-based charity providing healthy living advice: our record is lousy, yours is great – so you should take the lead.

The essence of Conservatism

So a truly modern party, making an honest assessment of each of the big challenges we face, will come inevitably to the conclusion that its agenda must reflect the notion of shared responsibility: that we're all in this together. We have a shared responsibility for our shared future.

We'll never achieve a dynamic economy and a decent society if we expect the government to do everything, as the left say, or if we expect individuals acting on their own to do everything, as some on the Right imply. Real modernisation means understanding that just as the Left is not sufficiently aware of the limitations of government, the Right has been too limited in its aspirations for government.

Of course we must talk about the limitations of government, but we must never be limited in our aspirations for government.

Shared responsibility is the hallmark of a civilised society. It's a profound Conservative insight and instinct that the state can't do everything and shouldn't try. We understand that everyone is different; that there are no simple, central solutions in politics. We're inherently optimistic about the human condition. We understand the desire and ability of people to better themselves and to do their best for their families and their communities. That's why we want to give them more responsibility. Shared responsibility is the essence of Conservatism.

So as we apply these timeless Conservative principles to address the challenge of today and tomorrow, I believe we have a great opportunity once again to inspire our country about what we can do to make it a better place in which to live.

"We'll never achieve a dynamic economy and a decent society if we expect the government to do everything"

But only if we apply the three tests: to hold fast to our fundamental beliefs and values. To think for the long-term. To develop ideas and policies that will work.

In an age of social fragmentation, where individuals and communities are often turning inwards to themselves, not outwards to each other, working together for the common good is the way to create a new and inspiring sense of national identity. That's what I mean by shared responsibility.

That's what will deliver the dynamic economy, the decent society, and the strong and self-confident nation that we all want to see.

We have spent much of the past eight years telling people what we are going to save them from. We now need to make clear what we wish to lead the country to. The empowered individual, the active community, the confident nation. I believe these mark the route to a Conservative victory.

Rt Hon Kenneth Clarke QC MP
Former Chancellor of the Exchequer

Ken was born in 1940 and is the Member of Parliament for Rushcliffe, a seat he has held since 1970.

Ken has wide-ranging cabinet level experience, having served as Secretary of State for Health, 1988-1990; Secretary of State for Education and Science 1990 -1992; Secretary of State for Home Office, 1992 – 1993; Chancellor of the Exchequer, 1993-1997.

Educated at Gonville and Caius College, Cambridge, he is a barrister-at-law and was called to the bar in 1963 and became a QC in 1980. He is married with two children.

Time is Running Out

Our Party will return to Government when it embraces the values of One Nation Conservatism and articulates the policies which flow from them. That means understanding and responding to the aspirations and concerns of the broad centre ground of the British nation. It means, in particular, a party which is tolerant not sectarian and which believes that the rights and opportunities of the individual must be enjoyed and must develop alongside, and where relevant, contribute to the well-being of the community.

One Nation politics has always rested upon four essential pillars: resolutely guarding against the incremental extension of state power and the excessive pre-emption of resources by the state; toleration towards the way people live their lives; vigilance in defence of civil liberties; and a broadly internationalist outlook when we address Britain's role in the world.

Since 1997 we have seemed to part company with some of the concerns of the British people. When we did begin to address issues of general concern too we sometimes did so in a way that suggested we were more concerned with ideology than with successful outcomes. Choice is an excellent principle but we became lost in the mechanics of "choice" rather than emphasising our commitment to first rate hospitals and schools.

Unfortunately, every piece of post-election analysis tells us that we were seen by the electorate as sectarian, composed of a small section of our society and interested exclusively in the welfare of that section. Large sections of the electorate were looking for an alternative to Labour: they did not turn to the Conservatives. They just did not see the Conservative Party as having any empathy with their situation.

> "Large sections of the electorate were looking for an alternative to Labour... they just did not see the Conservative Party as having any empathy with their situation"

Yet this is patently untrue in the real world beyond elections. The active citizen, working in the community to raise money for voluntary activities or to provide equipment for hospitals or fund hospices or play groups or Macmillan nurses or active in housing associations or regeneration partnerships is very likely to be a Conservative. There are

> "There are Conservative MPs who have won seats way down the "target" list because they were able to identify with the needs of the community"

Time is Running Out

Conservative MPs who have won seats way down the "target" list because they were able to identify with the needs of the community. We need to convince people that the Conservative Party nationally has at its heart the same commitment to working to improve the lives of everyone in this country as have the thousands of Conservatives who give their time to public and voluntary activities.

Easier said than done? Of course. But I believe that the party is better placed than it has been at any time since 1997 to re-assert the values and attitudes which took it to government- and kept it there- for the largest part of the post-war period. One reason for this is that the issue which has divided the party, sometimes bitterly, over the past decade need no longer be the cause of disunity. The European constitution is dead: I see no point in any attempt to resurrect it. Europe needs to concentrate on achieving competitiveness in the global economy so that it can generate jobs, investment, innovation and enterprise. This is the job overwhelmingly of the member states. As for the Euro I believe that the issue of British entry is dead for this parliament and the next and perhaps even longer.

> "The European constitution is dead: I see no point in any attempt to resurrect it"

This means that the two issues generating the most active division in the party are no longer on the agenda. The British public has, overwhelmingly, been either bored rigid by our internal debate on Europe or, worse, and carefully nurtured by Labour, seen it as evidence of the party's extremism. We should put this issue behind us.

The intervention in Iraq was a genuinely agonising issue. I believe firmly that the invasion was wrong and British participation a huge mistake. The present situation in Iraq which certainly flows in part from inadequate preparations for the post-Saddam pacification must give concern to us all – and especially to the families of the British servicemen doing such a dangerous and demanding job with immense professionalism and dedication. The Government must not be allowed to escape unchallenged on events in Iraq and how we can manage transition to full Iraqi control and the wider consequences of the intervention both for the region and for our own security against the threat of terrorism.

> "I believe firmly that the invasion was wrong and British participation a huge mistake"

This brings us squarely to the first thing we have to do: challenge

Rt Hon Ken Clarke QC MP

Labour effectively in the House and outside. The next election will be fought against Prime Minister Gordon Brown. It will not be easy- indeed it could be tougher than the 2005 election. The Labour disability in the shape of Tony Blair will have been removed and, Gordon Brown will hope, party disaffection over Iraq with it.

> "Unless we challenge Gordon Brown on the central issue of the economy... we will not get within sight of power"

Indeed, Brown will be telling the country that it has had a change of government. Unless we can challenge Gordon Brown on the central issue of the economy and show that we can deliver real value for tax-payers money we will not get within sight of power.

Gordon Brown has hectored, lectured and preached at us for eight years while presiding over huge increases in public spending which have delivered very poor value in terms of improving public services while vastly complicating the tax system, and the administration of benefits (ask those trying to make the tax credit system work!). Meanwhile business is buried under the burden of new Labour regulation- so much so that the competitive advantages that British business enjoyed are being seriously eroded. New Labour has boasted that it is "business-friendly" whilst we, if we are honest, can no longer take it for granted that we are the natural home of the business vote: we have to get out and work for it both by making a sustained attack on unnecessary regulation at national and European level and scrutinising every aspect of state spending so that we can create a freer environment for the private sector.

The past three elections were disastrous. Of course we won some magnificent individual victories last May but the overall picture was still very black. We have, in general, chased votes up the age scale, down the social-economic scale and into the South East. We trail behind both Labour and Liberal Democrats among the under 35 year old voters. It is not enough to "bring home"

> "We have in general chased votes up the age scale, down the socio-economic scale and into the South East"

the former Conservative voters: we have to create a whole new generation of first-time Conservative voters who see the party as the natural expression of their aspirations- and that means the hard-pressed Thirty-and-a-bit year olds struggling to get onto the housing ladder, pay off the debts from university, raise a family and, if we are honest, start contributing to a pension fund. And, on top of that, perhaps having to address the needs of elderly parents.

Time is Running Out

We tend to use the expression "lifestyle issues." In truth lifestyle issues are very often about hard economics and income – paying for child-care, the cost of commuting, the remoteness of public services. For many people the key to choice is cash and it is the fundamental instinct of Tory governments to maintain as low a tax burden as is compatible with the effective discharge of the state's responsibilities to all sections of the community.

> "For many people the key to choice is cash"

The party has suffered, particularly, from the erosion of our support to the Liberal Democrats. The fact that they did not have the triumph they expected at the general election – and that we made a handful of gains at their expense, does not disguise the alarming shift of support from traditionally Tory-inclined professional people to the Liberal Democrats. In fact I suspect that such Tory voters who defected to New Labour in 1997 migrated to the Liberal Democrats in May. I am convinced that we can regain the natural support of such groups because we offer the one thing which escapes the Liberals – the prospect of government. But we will only do so if we re-espouse the One Nation ideas and values with which they feel at home.

But we have only got one election to do so. If we are not able to enter the next election as a broadly-based party appealing across the spectrum – to the white collar as well as the white van voter- then I fear that we will be in the political ghetto for a generation.

We are told that voters do not want machine politicians. They seek something called "authenticity." They want independence, conviction, the ability to work together, accessibility, open-mindedness. The political witch-doctors sum this up as "narrative." We may not be instinctively comfortable with such soft-edged politics, partly because Parliament draws its life from debate and differentiation. Tony Blair has been very good at the soft-edged politics of media presentation, at empathising with people. Perhaps that is why he is dismissive of Parliament - perhaps the one place for which he feels no empathy!

The Conservatives need to do better than Labour. We need to combine clear policy choices, expressed in terms of how they respond to the needs of the nation, combined with an ability to stitch these policies together into a positive vision for Britain. We have spent much of the past eight years telling people what we are going to save them from. We now need to make clear what we wish to lead the country to. The empowered individual, the active community, the confident nation. I believe these mark the route to a Conservative victory.

Tories can hector Britain and niggle negatively away, which is largely what they've done for the past eight years, or they can face up to Britain as it is and try to define a relevant, resonant, Conservative message for the 21st century.

Andrew Cooper
Director of Populus

Andrew Cooper is Director of Populus, a polling, research and strategy consultancy. Prior to Populus he was Director of Strategy for the Conservative Party and Head of Research at the Social Market Foundation. He holds a BSc in Economics from the London School of Economics and is married with three children.

What does the Conservative Party stand for?

It took the Labour Party four successive election defeats before there was a critical mass within the Party willing to change enough to win again. How many defeats will it take the Conservatives to reach the same stage? Michael Howard's description of the 2005 election result the next morning as "a huge step forward for the Conservative Party" suggests that the answer is 'more than three'.

The Harvard psephologist Pippa Norris, reflecting on the Conservative Party's predicament in a seminal essay last year, concluded that: "As in therapy, the first step towards recovery is to recognise a problem. The second is summoning the will to change. Until these blinkers are stripped, it seems unlikely that the Conservatives will take the first steps towards restoring their electoral fortunes".

"As in therapy, the first step towards recovery is to recognise a problem. The second is summoning the will to change"

2005 was a fluky advance

The truth is that the 2005 election was a humiliating rejection of the Conservative Party – the third in succession.

For all of the manifest unpopularity of the Labour Government the Conservative vote rose in 2005 by a measly half of one % – and actually fell overall in Labour-held seats, which plainly the party must win back if it is ever to advance.

Over the last two elections the Labour Party has lost 9% – of the vote it got in 1997, yet the Conservative vote has risen by just 1.5%. Only a small fraction of those turning away from Labour are choosing to vote Conservative instead, even though many of them had been Tory voters before switching to Labour.

"Only a small fraction of those turning away from Labour are choosing to vote Conservative"

The Conservative Party came third at this year's election among voters under 35 – the age group among whom it did best in 1979. Its vote fell in half the regions of England, making it more than ever a Southern rump. Its support fell among ABC1s, historically the bedrock when it is winning – and also among women, who voted disproportionately Conservative in the 1980s and early 1990s.

What does the Conservative Party stand for?

For the second election running the Tories were saved by low turnout from an even more crushing defeat: of those who decided in the end not to vote all, 48% would have voted Labour, 23% Lib Dem and only 21% Conservative. Polling suggests that for most of these would-be Labour voters the decisive factor in opting not to vote was the certainty of a Labour victory and, for many, a desire not to give Tony Blair too big a majority.

Only 30% of voters said, on the eve of the election, that they were satisfied with the Labour Government. That ought to have been a sign that voters felt it was 'time for a change' – but the same small proportion, just 30%, wanted a Conservative government instead. The largest group of voters, about two in five, defined themselves as dissatisfied with the Blair Government but nevertheless preferred it to the Tory alternative. Labour were re-elected because most voters just couldn't face the thought of a Conservative government. It is hard to think of a more damning indictment.

Some will argue that the election of 32 more Conservative MPs in 2005 represents a step forward. But the Tories still have fewer than 200 MPs – a threshold that Michael Foot, the textbook case study in unelectability, managed easily to pass in 1983. And even the relatively small increase in the number of Tory MPs

"Of the 31 seats gained from Labour, 18 were won not because of voters switching from Labour to the Conservatives"

is less impressive than it looks. Of the 31 seats gained from Labour, 18 were won not because of voters switching from Labour to the Conservatives (indeed in some of these seats the Tory vote actually fell), but from Labour votes swinging to the Liberal Democrats (or, in some cases, the BNP).

The increased number of Tory MPs is, in other words, not a solid stride forward but a largely fluky advance that could easily be reversed at the next election, when the circumstances leading to the Iraq war will be a distant memory, Labour will have a new leader and many of those voting Lib Dem this time in protest may well revert to Labour. In 2005 most of the Liberal Democrat gains from Labour were seats which had been Tory-held before Labour won them; the Lib Dems have nearly caught the Conservatives in the number of seats where each party is second, and therefore the main local challenger, to Labour. The pendulum has not stopped; it has just stopped swinging to the Conservatives.

The Conservative Party's condition is not yet terminal, but the Party has now been in a persistent vegetative state for more than a decade. Intellectually comatose and asleep to the endless change in the world around it, the Tory Party has lain dormant through half a generation – ageing but otherwise utterly unaltered – waiting for some extreme combination of nostalgia about the past and disgruntlement about the present to revive it. Unless the Party awakens and finds within its belief system a proposition to resonate in Britain today it is likely to continue its drift towards irrelevance.

The Conservative Party has been behind Labour in the polls more or less continuously, barely flickering above its flat-line, since early 1993. It is necessary to look back that far and to view the Conservative Party from the voters' perspective to understand the party's predicament.

Politics of fear

The Conservatives won the 1992 election by successfully deploying what Bill Clinton terms 'the politics of fear'. People voted Tory to avert 'Labour's double whammy' – and because they couldn't bear the thought of Neil Kinnock as Prime Minister. Even then most voters rejected Labour only grudgingly since this meant putting up with a Conservative government that seemed to have lost the plot and run out of steam. In the event what unfolded in the years following that election was every bit as grim as the worst fears of how bad a Labour government would have been.

John Major put off the Tory day of reckoning for about as long as the law allowed. By the time he had to let the British people judge his government, the Conservative Party was as politically desperate as it was intellectually bankrupt. As the 1997 election campaign began, the Conservatives had even less to say for themselves than they had five years earlier. The only case for voting Tory that could be conceived was that new Labour meant 'New Danger'. But it turned out that not a single one of the awful things that the Tories said were sure to follow a Labour victory actually happened. Things didn't 'only get better' as dramatically as Labour had promised and voters had hoped, but the economy ticked over as steadily as ever, the Kingdom did not divide and the minimum wage and social chapter neither crippled business nor bankrupted Britain. New Labour, in fact, did not mean New Danger.

Four years later the Tory electoral message still showed no sign of recognising the obvious preference of most voters for a disappointing Labour government rather than an unchanged Conservative one – and still offered not a single positive reason to vote Conservative, ending the campaign rather pathetically

What does the Conservative Party stand for?

pleading with voters to 'burst Blair's bubble'.

The 2005 Conservative election campaign was just as relentlessly negative as the previous three. Reflexive blue collar whinges about Britain took the place of any positive argument for Conservative ideas – prefacing the ubiquitous question 'Are you thinking what we're thinking?' Polls found that the answer of more than two voters out of three was 'No'. Almost two thirds also thought that this year's Tory campaign was "mean, nasty and negative". The 2005 campaign thus failed tactically. More importantly it was a strategic disaster – trading away a further chunk of aspirational middle class professionals, whose votes have always been the real Tory core and who comprise a rapidly rising proportion of the electorate, in favour of a similar number of votes from unskilled workers and welfare dependents – groups that are diminishing in number, less likely to turn out to vote and hard completely to dislodge from a tribal economic loyalty to Labour. As a strategy it compounded the common confusion about the Conservative identity which the Party's policy positions have caused.

> "The 2005 campaign was a strategic disaster – trading away a further chunk of aspirational middle class professionals whose votes have always been the real Tory core"

Policies that reinforce negative perceptions

Two thirds of voters think that the Conservatives "just attack the government over whatever happens to be in the news and never say anything positive". More than half the electorate have simply concluded that "the Conservative Party doesn't seem to stand for anything at all anymore".

This is hardly surprising because it is virtually a generation since the Conservative Party based its electoral appeal on a positive vision of a better Britain. This fact is at the very root of the Party's decline. It has long been hard for the casual observer to work out what the point is of the Conservatives. And the truth is that there is remarkably little consensus among Tories on this point. What does the Conservative Party stand for? What is its vision? The Conservative Party's deepest problem is that it no longer has a unifying purpose.

> "It is virtually a generation since the Conservative Party based its electoral appeal on a positive vision of a better Britain"

In the absence of a broader vision of society and lacking a coherent theory about how to manage the state – as opposed to a non-specific belief that the state is too big – more and more

Conservatives have ended up concluding that "if we're not a party of tax cuts, we're a party of nothing". Tax obviously is an important issue for any party. But in today's Conservative Party it has swelled out of all proportion. For want of anything else substantial to say the Conservative Party has imposed on itself an obligation – partly just in order to justify its existence – to advance not just the general case for a lower rather than higher tax burden, but, at all times and in all circumstances, the specific case for tax cuts now. It is ironic that this point is generally advanced in the name of 'Thatcherism' since Margaret Thatcher herself, when in opposition, made no promise to cut taxes and clearly understood that tax cuts, in isolation of a broader narrative and vision, are neither a necessary nor a sufficient condition for a Conservative majority.

The Tory fixation with the issue of tax is evidence of another critical problem too: the tendency always to talk about the things Conservatives think are important, rather than addressing the concerns of the mass of voters whose support must be gained if an election is ever to be won.

Like it or not, polls clearly tell us that tax is nowhere near the top of voters' concerns. Even more significantly, even if tax was a salient issue, bitter experience has taught voters that there is no rational reason to believe politicians promising tax cuts. It is a central conceit of Tories that tax cuts are part of the Party's core DNA, but this is not a perception shared by voters, who have learned to judge parties by what they do, not what they say. The Conservative Party increased taxes in government when it had promised not to, and in opposition has been defined by tactical opportunism and persistent negativism, neither of which inclines people to feel it can be taken at its word.

"Like it or not, polls clearly tell us that tax is nowhere near the top of voters' concerns"

As Michael Portillo has written, "the worst error you can make in politics is to believe the electorate thinks the same as your party". The most basic lesson of three heavy election defeats is that the Conservative Party must engage with the issues that concern ordinary voters.

On almost every conceivable measure the third of the country that votes Tory has a different outlook from the two thirds that do not.

During the election Conservative supporters were more than twice as likely as non-Conservatives to regard immigration or tax as the most important issue. Non-Conservatives were more than

What does the Conservative Party stand for?

twice as likely as Tory voters to view pensions, social security, the NHS or the economy as the most important issue. Agreement that "Britain was a better country to live in 20 or 30 years ago" is 36% higher among those who voted Conservative in May than among those who didn't.

Of all the devastating evidence in Michael Ashcroft's 'wake-up call to the Conservative Party', published a month after the election, the most devastating are the graphs showing that Tory pronouncements which had the most positive impact on the enthusiasm of Conservative voters also had the most negative impact on floating voters – as if Tories and non-Tories inhabit not only different worlds, but ones which are polar opposites. As a result nearly eight out of ten Conservative voters think that the party is "on the right track to get back into power before long", while barely a quarter of non-Tories think so. Most Tories think the party doesn't need to change at all, just to "stick to its guns and put over its existing policies with more vigour"; only one non-Tory in eight agrees, while four times as many think the Conservative Party "needs to change significantly" if it is to stand any chance of winning again.

> "Tory pronouncements which had the most positive impact on the enthusiasm of Conservative voters also had the most negative impact on floating voters"

The Conservative Party, however, shows every sign of not wanting to change and of understanding neither why nor how it should. Tories are reminiscent of the mindset Dick Morris found among congressional Democrats after that party's crushing defeat in the 1994 mid-term elections: "they acted as if the last election never happened, so much so that I wondered whether they imagined their defeat had been a mere typographical error. It was as if they were waiting for a recount to restore their mandate". This reflects a surprising failure to comprehend one of the basic rules of politics – of human psychology in fact. After defeat political parties must "concede and move on" as Philip Gould termed it in Labour's context. Or, as Michael Portillo puts it "a party that loses has to tell the voters they were right to reject it, It must change. It is the change that permits the electorate to give it another chance". For, as Portillo concluded, "If a party does not change, then voters are implicitly being required to say they were the ones who got it wrong. The Conservatives by their body language look to be waiting for the voters to realize their terrible mistake".

But Britain did not reject the Conservative Party three times in a row by accident. Voters are not the slightest bit sorry about it – for most people judge the party unelectable. No matter how deeply unpopular Labour may become the British people will never be persuaded that they were wrong to kick out and keep rejecting the Tories – any more than the collective desire to expunge the Conservatives in 1997 made voters regret electing Tory governments through the 1980s. It is high time Tories faced the depths of their predicament honestly and reflected candidly on the causes.

For a party in opposition, policies are illustrative of values, not an end in themselves. People do not pore over the detail of different parties' policies weighing up their comparative merits (though many pretend they do). Voters piece together a sense of the values and ideals of a party from numerous fragments – sound-bites on the news, headlines in the paper, snippets of speeches, positions taken on passing issues, leaflets through the door. Correlation analysis of poll data reveals that the single best predictor of whether or not someone votes Conservative is if they agree that "the Conservative Party shares my values"; values should be the thread that all of a party's words and actions have in common. Voters struggle to evaluate the things that parties say they'll do, so they tend to defer to a conception of a party's motives and its aspirations. Consistently only 34% of voters think the Tories share their values – 20% lower than the equivalent figure for Labour and the Lib Dems, meaning that those parties have a much bigger pool of potential voters. The general perception of Tory values is bleak. Two thirds of voters think the Conservative Party is "out of touch". 58% think the Tories "don't care about ordinary people". Just over half think Conservatives "care more about protecting the interests of the well - off than they do about the have-nots". The same proportion thinks the party is simply "stuck in the past". Nearly half believe that Conservatives are "narrow - minded and bigoted".

"Voters piece together a sense of the values and ideals of a party from numerous fragments – sound bites on the news, headlines in the paper, positions on passing issues…"

Coming to terms with modern Britain

The Conservative Party must, finally, come, to terms with modern Britain. Margaret Thatcher laid most of its foundations; as Peter Jenkins wrote, presciently, in 1987, "the future may not be hers, but she has set its agenda". Millions of people voted for her Conservative Governments because her vision of popular capitalism represented a liberating conviction that people have the right to be all they can be. Today the Conservatives seem to resent

What does the Conservative Party stand for?

the end-result of the liberating principles unleashed in the 1980s; for a party whose axiom of default is 'trust the people', many Tories are remarkably quick to judge the way that people choose now to live their lives.

When Tories get together and talk about Britain, what often unfolds is one vast harrumph about what Britain has become. Rather than reach out to a mass market, the Conservative Party has seemed content to become the campaigning arm of the Daily Mail, fanzine of 1950s Britain and, it must be remembered, an institution that, unlike the Conservative Party, can go on forever while appealing only to a hard core of a few million nostalgics.

> "for a party whose axiom of default is 'trust the people', many Tories are remarkably quick to judge the way that people live their lives"

It has often been remarked that the Tory Party needs to look more like Britain but it has remained overwhelmingly a white party of grumpy old people which, at best, patronises women, gays and ethnic minorities. With no vision for a better future, the Conservative Party has come to represent little more than the last stand of yesterday over tomorrow. If it is ever to win again the Conservative Party must move on from the past and work out what its unifying purpose is in a country whose liberal values cannot be disputed and therefore must be either embraced or confronted.

Two thirds of voters, for example, think that gay couples should have "exactly the same rights" as heterosexual couples. A formerly ostracised community has become an accepted part of the mainstream of society. How are voters to judge politicians who claim to 'trust the people' but then want to stigmatize gays? Where, people may wonder, is the intellectual coherence of a 'Conservative' party which bristles at gays who, as Andrew Sullivan has described, when allowed to do so by the lifting of state sanctions against them, 'claim not simply sexual freedom but also the responsibilities of military service and civil marriage'.

70% of voters believe that "it is not a matter for political parties to express a preference between marriage, and couples living together outside marriage". Many – probably most – Conservatives disagree, and 'support for marriage' remains a totemic principle for a lot of Tories, even now. But voters think that the priority for any government should be to support 'hardworking families' and many will find it hard to vote for a party that chooses to discriminate between families on the basis of whether or not their relationship has been consecrated by the state.

Andrew Cooper

More than three quarters of voters think that 'the single change that would most improve life in Britain today is people being more tolerant of different ethnic groups and cultures'. It is scarcely surprising that the relentlessness of the Conservative campaign focus on immigration, asylum and gypsies struck the wrong chord.

Both the changing demographics of Britain and every measure there is of the country's anxieties and values scream out for a different kind of Conservative Party. Tories can hector Britain and niggle negatively away, which is largely what they've done for the past eight years, or they can face up to Britain as it is and try to define a relevant, resonant, Conservative message for the 21st century. Time is running out. If the Conservative Party does not change, it will die.

In an age when people are accustomed to making a range of choices in their daily lives, it is perverse that one sphere in which such choices are denied is the public realm. Rather than sitting in London and dictating to people, we must look to push power down as far as possible so that ordinary people can exercise it for themselves.

Rt Hon David Davis MP
Shadow Home Secretary

David Davis was born in 1948 and is the Member of Parliament for Haltemprice and Howden. He extended his previously slim majority of just 2,000 to over 5,000 in the 2005 General Election despite a Liberal Democrat decapitation strategy to unseat him. David has served as the Chairman of the Commons Public Accounts Committee and was a candidate in the 2001 leadership contest from which he withdrew after the second ballot. He was MP for Boothferry from 1987 to 1997. He has been Shadow Home Secretary since 2003 and was a Minister of State in the Foreign & Commonwealth Office in John Major's Government.

Educated at Warwick University and London Business School, David was a Director of Tate & Lyle plc before entering Parliament. He is married to Doreen and they have three children.

Power to the People

By the time the next election comes, the Conservative Party will in all likelihood have been in opposition for twelve years.

If we are to ensure we don't remain there, we will have to achieve something over the next four years that we have singularly failed to do over the past eight: we will have to become a credible alternative government of Britain.

Perhaps it was the natural consequence of being in government for so long, but when the voters rejected us in 1997 we were lost and bemused. Many people began to ask searching questions about the future of the Conservative Party, even calling into question the very values on which the Party was founded in the mid-19th century.

> "In the midst of the polarising debate, it is hardly surprising that we failed to devise a credible programme for government"

Some people asked whether those values were out of date today and suggested that 'Blairism' had forever changed the political landscape of Britain. They argued that the Conservative Party would only win again when it had learned to be more like Mr Blair and New Labour.

On the other side of the coin were those who argued that we needed 'clear blue water' between the parties and that all we Conservatives needed to do was complete the Thatcherite revolution.

In the midst of this polarising debate, it is hardly surprising that we failed to devise a credible programme for government.

Eventually we learned how to be a good opposition, but too often we forgot about the need to stake out a clear alternative based on Conservative values that, far from being transient, are in fact timeless.

That is the key task of the Conservative Party over the course of the next Parliament.

The Britain we live in

To begin to apply timeless Conservative principles to the problems of today, we must first ensure we understand precisely what those problems are.

In short, we must have a proper understanding of the country in which we live.

More properly, we must understand that it is in fact two nations – the haves and the have-nots.

Power to the People

Life for some people in Britain today is comfortable. They are well-educated, financially stable and socially secure. These are the people who are able to take advantage of the opportunities life throws up.

> "But for many ordinary people, daily life is a struggle. These are the have-nots – Britain's second nation – the people I call the victims of state failure"

They would, of course, like things to be better still – and they have generally grown weary of Mr Blair's endless taxes and broken promises – but they have benefited the most from the Conservative reforms of the 1980s and 90s and agree that Britain is a far better place today than it was thirty years ago.

But for many ordinary people, daily life is still a struggle.

They struggle to meet the mortgage repayments and to pay the bills on time. They struggle to balance the demands of work and home. They struggle too with their family life and worry about whether their son or daughter is getting on well in school and whether the health service will be there for them if they fall ill.

These are the have-nots – Britain's second nation – the people I call the victims of state failure.

Two nations of Labour's making

The cause of this divide is a lack of opportunity in British society, yet the Labour Party's policies are making it worse.

We need to understand this point if we are to set out a clear, Conservative alternative.

Take, for example, today's rigid structures in health and education. By defending them with such force, the Labour Government is denying to the less well off the opportunities that are open to the fortunate few.

> "In today's rigged market of state education only the rich can exercise choice"

Think about the health service. In trying to get into a good hospital, the middle classes are generally more adept at finding the requisite information and making the necessary contacts than are less self-assured working class people.

Moreover, as Professor Julian Le Grand, the Prime Minister's Policy Strategy Adviser, observed last November, it's the richer and better educated people who actually make most use of the health system. Not surprisingly, then, poor people have worse health outcomes. For example, in 38 of 43 types of cancer analysed, it's been shown that the survival rates of the affluent are greater than those of the least well off.

In education, the divide is probably even greater. OFSTED consistently reports that the lowest school standards are concentrated in the most deprived areas. This isn't because children from poorer families are stupider, or their parents less committed. It's because in today's rigged market of state education only the rich can exercise choice. Wealthier people can buy a house in a good school's catchment area; poorer people can't afford to move.

One recent study suggested that the premium on a house in the best possible secondary school area, compared with the worst, stands at £23,700. In these circumstances, it is impossible to describe state education as truly free.

An opportunity agenda

So the Conservative Party's agenda for government must be an opportunity agenda.

This is a timeless Conservative value. It is what Churchill meant when he spoke of a Britain in which "there is a limit beneath which no man may fall, but no limit to which any man might rise".

A belief in the freedom of the individual lies at the heart of Conservatism. We believe that people will always make better decisions for themselves than any politician or bureaucrat ever will. That is precisely why a modern Conservative agenda for government must focus on opening up opportunities, so that we are able to break through the glass ceilings in British society and move towards the One Nation ideal to which we aspire.

> "The first thing for us to do is to recognise and argue that opportunity flourishes when the economy thrives, and that the best economies are low tax, light regulation economies"

And there are some specific paths the modern Conservative Party should follow to achieve it.

Opportunity flourishes when the economy thrives

The first thing for us to do is to recognise and argue that opportunity flourishes when the economy thrives, and that the best economies are low tax, light regulation economies.

They promote opportunity in three ways.

Firstly, they create jobs. You only need to look at the difference between the US and much of Europe to see that this is true. The high tax, high regulation, European model has led to twice as high unemployment as the system which makes America the most powerful economy in the world.

This is important because a job gives someone both dignity and financial reward. A job is the most effective antidote to poverty and the lack of a job is the most obvious barrier to opportunity.

Secondly, they create the wealth on which so much depends. A thriving economy pays for hospitals, schools, roads, and police. Low tax economies can thus sustain better services, and higher levels of spending, than high tax economies.

Third, low tax, free enterprise economies encourage the virtues required if a modern society is to flourish and be truly fluid. A functioning free enterprise economy, under a rule of law, encourages the qualities we need to make society work: self-reliance, hard work, independence of mind, a spirit of cooperation, pride of ownership, personal responsibility, and generosity.

These qualities enable people to make the most of the opportunities that come their way.

Security is a prerequisite of opportunity

A second task we face is that of building a secure society.

Britain is an increasingly insecure country. We face threats from home and abroad. The age of international terrorism is with us, while the rule of law sometimes seems to have given way to the rule of the mob at home.

Violent crime is up by 90%, and robberies by 50%, since Labour took office. Persistent youth offending has risen. Cocaine use has trebled.

Meanwhile, detection rates have fallen. There are 900,000 more unsolved crimes each year than there were in 1998. The signals from the Government about use of drink and drugs, which both fuel crime, have been disastrous.

The better off have a reasonable chance of escaping the consequences of this breakdown of law and order. Their houses are barred and alarmed. They travel everywhere by car. Their neighbourhoods are safer.

"Britain is an increasingly insecure country. We face threats from home and abroad. The rule of law sometimes seems to have given way to the rule of the mob at home"

It is the less well off who suffer most. They are more likely to be burgled. Their cars are more likely to be stolen. And unemployed people are twice as likely to be victims of violent crime.

So we have to strengthen the forces of law and order. The police should feel confident in their capacity to enforce the law, free from political interference and politically correct policies that hold them back. Zero tolerance policing, like that used so successfully in New York and at home here in Middlesbrough, should be encouraged and made wide-spread.

Prisons must be made more productive, with proper rehabilitation regimes so that crime rates fall over the long-term.

And we must also give greater focus to ensuring criminals are brought to justice speedily and to making the criminal justice system as transparent as possible.

Finally, we must put in place proper, long-term strategies for tackling some of the causes of crime such as alcohol and drug abuse. Much of this can be done not by government, but by voluntary groups or charities whose success rate in dealing with these issues is so often better than those of programmes run by the state.

Extending opportunity by putting people in control

A further path towards achieving our One Nation ideal is that of empowering individuals.

In an age when people are accustomed to making a range of choices in their daily lives, it is perverse that the one sphere in which such choices are denied is the public realm.

If we are genuinely to extend opportunity to the many, not just the few, we will have to argue for a new political settlement – one in which decisions are taken as close to the people they effect as possible.

"Rather than sitting in London and dictating to people, we must look to push power down as far as possible so that ordinary people can exercise it for themselves"

Politicians must accept that they are no longer held in the regard they once were. Rather than sitting in London and dictating to people, we must look to push power down as far as possible so that ordinary people can exercise it for themselves.

In policing, for example, this would involve a transfer of power to local police chiefs who would be directly elected by the communities they serve. They would then be forced to set the policing priorities that local people want to see.

But this fundamental change in the way we conduct politics in Britain could be even more radical when it comes to the public services like health and education.

Extending opportunity by reforming the public services

Our health service and education system remain the key areas in which ordinary people have too little control over the outcomes they enjoy.

Too often, people are forced to take what they are given and, because they have no choice other than to accept it, what they are given is rarely good enough.

As I stated above, the fortunate few can afford to buy their way out of this counsel of despair. The Conservative Party must commit itself to extending that opportunity to the many who do not enjoy such luxuries.

We must therefore be unstinting in making the case for reform in the public services. Offering more of the same 'managerialism' simply won't do. It is time for change.

We must demonstrate how ending the state's monopoly on provision, empowering people to take control and scrapping the centrally dictated targets that make our schools and hospitals dance to the Government's tune will ensure that everyone has the opportunity to access the very best services imaginable.

If they do it in other modern European countries, we can do it here too.

Supporting the family as an institution

Finally, an incoming Conservative government will have to address some of the long-term problems that contribute to our polarised society.

We cannot turn our face away from those who have fallen on hard times financially or emotionally. Our economic liberalism must be matched by a renewed commitment to activism when we believe the government could and should help those in need.

> "Our economic liberalism must be matched by a renewed commitment to activism when we believe the Government could and should help those in need"

Many of the problems in British society today stem from family breakdown. The family has become undervalued as an institution in Britain today, yet it is in the interests of all – single, married, black, white, young, old, gay or straight – to keep the traditional family strong. It is necessary for our economic success and for our stability as a nation. If the family fails, society falls.

There is a growing, and welcome, consensus in the Conservative Party on these matters. Over the next four years we must devise and pursue policies that will reverse the decline on the family's status in British society.

By doing so we will ensure the social structures are in place to enable people to make the most of the opportunities that come their way.

A new Tory idealism

At the next election, it is probable that the Conservative Party will be facing a man who has done more than any other New Labour politician to build the glass ceilings that exist in British society today.

Gordon Brown, through his heavy-handed, intrusive, high-tax, high-regulation policies has created a stagnant society in which a fortunate few can succeed while those at the bottom continue to struggle.

We now have four years in which to set out a credible alternative agenda for government; four years in which to make ourselves the champions of opportunity for all.

That must be our driving ideal: the long-held Conservative ideal of building One Nation.

We will only achieve it by reaching beyond the polarising extremes of left and right, modern and traditional, and applying the best of timeless Conservative thinking to the problems of today.

In the past the Party has overcome economic decline, and as a result Britain changed, and our opponents changed, but we did not change we became victims of our own success.

Alan Duncan MP
Shadow Secretary of State for Transport

Alan Duncan was born in 1957 and has been the Member of Parliament for Rutland and Melton since 1992. Alan has been a Shadow Minister across a range of portfolios including, Health, Trade & Industry, Foreign & Commonwealth Affairs; Constitutional Affairs, and International Development. He has been Shadow Secretary of State for Transport since May 2005.

Educated at Oxford and Harvard, where he was a Kennedy Scholar, Alan worked for Shell Petroleum, and subsequently for an independent commodity company as a trader of crude oil and refined products. He owned his own oil broking and advisory company before entering Parliament.

He was President of the Oxford Union in 1979.

Get Real or Die

Any political party needs a cause. When underpinned by a clear body of interest it stands the chance, historically, of being able to win elections. The Liberals lost their base a century ago, as Labour harnessed the newly enfranchised workers' vote, and we now face the prospect of losing ours as we become detached from the composition and complexion of the country we think we should govern.

Labour has cleverly detected the significance of changing social patterns in Britain, and has harnessed a new coalition of interests which, so far, has served it well. Conservatives, in contrast, have hardly even begun to ask themselves where our future support will be drawn from, because too many still fail to appreciate the perilous erosion of our political base.

"I want a Britain that is socially liberal and economically liberal. I believe people should be free to live as they choose until they do harm to others and fail to meet their responsibilities"

I would love a country in which people are politely devout, never divorce or abort, and loyally wave the Union Jack. But blimpish adherence to this image of yesteryear as a foundation for our politics today would condemn us to growing irrelevance and ridicule. Politicians have to address society as it is, and not perpetuate the illusions of a bygone age.

A socially and economically liberal Britain

I want a Britain that is socially liberal and economically liberal. I believe people should be free to live as they choose until they do harm to others and fail to meet their responsibilities. I believe that a low tax economy in which the state does less and people do more for themselves is ultimately more free, more prosperous and more moral. But politics is the art of the possible, and in a democracy if you don't get the votes, you don't get the key to Number 10, and at the moment we do not inspire confidence.

Our support has hardly shifted for a decade, and our apparent gains at the last election were largely the perverse by-product of a straight switch in support from Labour to the Lib Dems. The support we do enjoy is predominantly male, elderly and rural, and amongst the under 35s

"Calamitously, through a combination of a vicious cycle of economic ups and downs followed by bailing out of the ERM, we sacrificed our unique selling point: economic competence"

Get Real or Die

we are in third place.

The foundations of our previous success in government were laid 30 years ago, and served us and Britain well for over a decade in office. Our philosophy and policies were in tune with voters' deepest concerns, and successive Conservative governments rescued Britain from economic humiliation. But we became victims of our own success. We overcame economic decline, and as a result Britain changed, and our opponents changed, but we did not. Then calamitously, through a combination of a vicious cycle of economic ups and downs followed by bailing out of the ERM, we sacrificed our unique selling point: economic competence. If the Tories can't handle the money, why bother with them? Ironically, seven years of Labour government have produced an economic backdrop which to most people is fundamentally benign: they can all pay the bills. They just don't realise the enormity of the confidence trick being played on them by Labour's criminal raid on tomorrow's pensions to pay for today's votes.

> "People don't realise the enormity of the confidence trick being played on them by Labour's criminal raid on tomorrow's pensions to pay for today's votes."

Aspiration, fair-mindedness and charisma

Much of the leadership debate has focused on trends and philosophy, and there is no doubt that we need a new battle of ideas through which to reassert our beliefs so as to persuade a new generation of voter. But politics is also about practicality. In modern elections, the messenger matters as much as the message. And the imagery (such as it is) and personality of the Conservative Party at the moment fail to persuade: 'dated, selfish and humourless' say those I speak to in schools. But this is easily remedied if our MPs in particular appreciate the task.

So where do we go from here? To put the Conservative Party back on the road we need three crucial ingredients: aspiration, fair-mindedness and charisma. Our vision of Britain should include measures which make everyone feel their interests and hopes lie with us. A Conservative view of poverty, which expresses genuine indignation at the plight of those stuck in housing estates without ambition or self-esteem, should be emblazoned on our reputation. We have failed to challenge the Left by asking what we should teach and how we

> "Charisma, like leadership, cannot be taught. You've either got it or you haven't"

should teach it. One simple policy which could transform the social deterioration of British society is to reduce primary school classes to no more than 20. Catch them young and keep order in class so they learn, and so much would change for the better.

We must restore our reputation for economic competence with an honest assessment of how we can build long-term financial stability for families across the cycle of their spending life including the growing burdens of old age. Philosophy and practicality converge – perhaps clash – when it comes to tax cuts. Yes, we want them and believe in them, but we need to persuade people to that view by first removing their fear of the consequences.

Fair-mindedness is a powerful force. Brash political combat may satisfy the participants, and win strident headlines, but it is not often a technique in persuasion. The Conservative Party needs to be so reasonable nobody need feel the urge to vote Liberal Democrat. In the past during the tenure of a Labour government, the Conservatives would enjoy a resurgence and the Liberals would crumble. Not so now. As we face an increasingly self-evident three-cornered fight, we risk further decline if we do not amend our techniques to woo the protest vote we have habitually pushed in the direction of the Lib Dems.

> "As we approach the long-awaited choice of leader we need simple concepts and ruthless practicality"

Charisma, like leadership, cannot be taught. You've either got it or you haven't. It is an essential ingredient for modern political success, and without it we are restrained. With it is needed the full force of party organisation, language crafting and TV imagery.

We've been through a few months of soul-searching. We've drawn all the historical parallels, and played around with concepts of liberalism and authoritarianism. We have always been a pragmatic party too. As we approach the long-awaited choice of leader we need simple concepts and ruthless practicality. With a united party behind such efforts, the next Conservative leader will be the next Conservative Prime Minister.

The party has lost the support of too many women, too many young people, and too many opinion formers. Anyone with a social conscience has clearly found it a struggle to vote Conservative in the past few elections; we have to reverse that by appealing to all parts of society with a new expression of One Nation Conservatism.

Damian Green MP

Damian Green was born in 1956 and has been the Member of Parliament for Ashford since 1997. Damian has been a spokesperson for the Conservative Party in a number of roles including Education, Employment and Environment. He has served as the Shadow Secretary of State for Education and Skills and the Shadow Secretary of State for Transport.

Educated at Oxford, where he was President of the Oxford Union, Damian was a financial journalist and worked in the No 10 Policy Unit prior to his entry into politics.

He is Chairman of Parliamentary Mainstream and a Vice-President of the Tory Reform Group. He is married with two daughters.

There is Such a Thing as Society

Since our third election defeat last May everyone who has contributed to the debate on the future of the Conservative Party has at least agreed on one thing: we cannot carry on as before. There, of course, the agreement ends. Over the past few months I have listened to ultra-modernisers saying that we must become sensitive to the needs of a more metrosexual society, and ultra-traditionalists arguing that faith, flag and family should be our guiding lights.

"Speaking from the Party's moderate wing, it seems necessary for the Conservative Party to re-invent One Nation Conservatism for modern Britain."

Re - inventing One Nation Conservatism

My own proposal is an ambitious one. Speaking from the Party's moderate wing, it seems necessary for the Conservative Party to re-invent One Nation Conservatism for modern Britain. Tony Blair has proved that the party that is most associated with policies and attitudes which seek to unite rather than divide is likely to win elections. The Liberal Democrats, or at least their non-loopy wing, recognise the same truth. Since the Conservatives succeeded for a long time by starting from One Nation presumptions we can do so again.

To achieve this we need to recognise that this does mean simply continuing what the Blair Government has done, and nor does it mean revisiting the policies of past One Nation Conservative eras. The party has lost the support of too many women, too many young people, and too many opinion formers. Anyone with a social conscience has clearly found it a struggle to vote Conservative in the past few elections; we have to reverse that.

This is not only the right thing to do, it is electorally necessary. Others, notably Michael Ashcroft and Policy Exchange, have gone into the disturbing detail of where we went wrong at the last election, so I will concentrate on only one of the groups we ought to regard as part of our core vote: women. We will never win an election without a plurality of the women's vote. According to the Fawcett Society, immigration ranks fourth among women voters in issues they care about, behind childcare, education, and care for the elderly. The Conservative Party will surprise the electorate in a positive way when it puts up hand-written posters about how it plans to improve long-term care.

There is Such a Thing as Society

We need to start with general principles that provide the test against which all policies will be judged. If we have simple, clear principles we will be seen to be following our chosen path, and not simply reacting to events. To show that we have changed, some of these principles need to surprise people, in the way that new Labour surprised everyone by emphasising economic stability.

As our three principles, I would propose Opportunity, Community, and Internationalism. The latter two may sound strange on Tory lips, but they should not do so. Strong communities are necessary if we are not to accept that if an individual has a problem the only place he or she can turn for help is to the state, and the first and most important community is the family. Internationalism was once an attitude of mind that the Conservative Party would have regarded as normal.

> "As our three principles, I would propose Opportunity, Community, and Internationalism"

We need a new expression of One Nation Conservatism, because the modern policies which flow from accepting One Nation ideals are market-oriented, anti-statist, and in many cases traditionally associated with the right rather than the left of the Conservative Party. There is a new idealistic consensus available to the Tory Party which will help the disadvantaged by using the power of competition and voluntary association. We can achieve One Nation goals by pursuing liberal free market methods.

An opportunity society

Take Opportunity first. I take it as a basic Conservative proposition that anyone should be able to fulfil their ambitions, wherever they start from, if they have the capacity. When I hear Labour politicians talk about our class-ridden society I ponder at what point I stopped being a boy born in a terraced house in a small town in South Wales, educated in state schools, and became a privileged middle-class Oxford graduate of the sort you expect to become a Tory politician. The fact is it should be an unremarkable journey, and I want a Britain in which it will remain unremarkable.

To achieve this, we need excellent education to be available to as many as possible. Tony Blair's education policy has failed to deliver the spread of educational excellence, despite an enormous increase in public spending. The solution is to empower parents – to give real choice to those who can't afford it out of their own income. In other words, to give the money the state spends on a child's education to the parent, and allow new bodies to set up state schools in which this money can be spent.

The One Nation element I would introduce would be to start the scheme in our inner cities, where the biggest challenges lie, and where, in practical terms, the ability to shift to a new school is greatest. So the first beneficiaries of new ideas would be those who have least choice, and least chance, at present.

Another policy which would help provide more opportunity for those struggling to do the right thing involves tax reform. Too many people are paying tax when they are barely earning enough to survive, and higher rate tax cuts in at levels where those paying cannot possibly be regarded as the rich. If the next Conservative government has any ability to cut taxes, then it should make sure that it helps those who are working hard to stay on their own feet.

Strength in communities

Community is my second, more surprising (for a Tory) principle. In today's world to be a successful independent individual you need a strong community around you. I want to see many layers between the state and the individual, and it is the multiplicity of communities to which any individual can belong, whether geographically based, interest groups, work-based or leisure oriented, which a good Conservative will encourage.

The most important community is the family, and the family is the most important support network for children. So One Nation Conservatives should be entirely happy to support policies which help children grow up with two parents in a stable relationship, and using the tax system to help married couples with children is one obvious way to achieve that.

> "In today's world to be a successful independent individual you need a strong community around you. I want to see many layers between the state and the individual."

Politicians should not preach about individual's relationships. We are not paid to do so and in many cases we are not fit to do so. But we are paid to encourage behaviour which helps create a better society.

Another policy area under the heading of community is the need for more local power. Elected mayors and even police chiefs would become big figures in their own right if they were given proper responsibilities. This would include a large degree of control over their own finances, which would entail a reduction in the grip of the Treasury over every penny spent by the public sector.

Internationalism

My third principle is Internationalism. We should be generous

There is Such a Thing as Society

minded and outward looking. First we should contribute a distinctive Tory voice to the increasingly important debate on debt relief and other anti-poverty measures. Secondly, we should take the current chaos at the heart of the EU as an opportunity. There is a constructive Conservative role to play inside the EU as the champion of reforming economics in alliance with many of the new members. There is no reason why we should not set out an alternative constitution to the one that is now failing, which British Conservatives could map out with colleagues from centre-right parties across the EU.

If Conservatives are to set themselves up as a plausible alternative government we need to offer hope. That hope will come if millions more people find they have control over their lives, and if a Conservative Britain can be confident and generous in our relationships with the rest of Europe and the world beyond. Not only must we stick to our principles but we need to be a crusading party, ready to fight for the improvements in the lives of ordinary people which the present Government has failed to deliver, for all its good intentions. After three Parliaments it will be obvious that the high-tax high-spend centralist model which New Labour has used for its own attempt at One Nation politics has failed. The chance for is to show that the same goals can be better achieved with our principles. When we can do this, we will be ready for government again.

> "After three Parliaments it will be obvious that the high-tax high-spend centralist model which New Labour has used for its own attempt at One Nation politics has failed"

So the first and overwhelmingly important task that the Conservative Party has to face up to is to restore people's faith in us as politicians. Nothing short of a revolution and a focus on what is in the best interests of Britain will be enough to halt the decline in the party's fortunes.

Nick Gibb MP
Shadow Minister for Education & Young People

Nick Gibb was born in 1960 and has been the Member of Parliament for Bognor Regis & Littlehampton since 1997. Nick was a frontbench spokesman on Trade and Industry matters between 1999 and 2001. He has been active since his election to the House of Commons with several Select Committee memberships to his name (Social Security, Treasury, Public Accounts, and Education & Skills).

Educated at Durham University with an honours degree in law, Nick was a Chartered Accountant with KPMG specializing in corporate taxation before entering parliament. He was an aide to Cecil Parkinson in the 1987 General Election.

Talking About a Revolution

Too few Conservatives understand the depth of the problem facing the Party. The fillip the 2005 election provided, with 33 extra seats, camouflaged the depressing reality that our 33% share of the vote has remained largely unchanged since we began flat-lining in the polls 12 years ago. A more detailed analysis of the polls reveals further horrors. We are in third place in the under-35 age group and if trends continue this will become the under-40 age group by the time of the next election. Our support among ABs has fallen by 3% since 2001.

"Those who believe the pendulum will swing back in the course of time are engaged in wishful thinking"

Nothing short of a revolution in the way we conduct politics and the approach we take to policy will be sufficient to halt our party's continual decline. Those who believe the pendulum will swing back in the course of time are engaged in wishful thinking. Those who believe that our salvation lies in the fact that the economy is about to implode overlook the fact that an independent Bank of England will counter any fiscal imprudence by Gordon Brown through its conduct of monetary policy. There is also the nagging question that even if the economy did suffer, why would this automatically result in support shifting to the Conservative Party? Our poll rating on economic competence still languishes far behind that of Labour.

When Conservatives reach for the tax cutting mantra as the root to power, they overlook the fact that despite a number of tax rises since 1997 (few of which surprised the electorate), interest rates are so low relative to the recent past that disposable incomes for middle-income households with a mortgage are significantly higher than in the 1990s. Which is why tax as a political issue rarely rises above 5th or 6th in the list of people's main political concerns.

"Conservatives overlook the fact that despite a number of tax rises since 1997…tax as a political issue rarely rises above 5th or 6th in the list of people's main political concerns"

Identifying the key issues

The issues that do register as worries are: the health service - almost always overwhelmingly the number one concern in the polls -, education (usually there at number two) and then crime. These are the issues that determined the outcome of the last two general elections and were a significant factor in our defeat in

Talking About a Revolution

1997. Unless the current government successfully reforms these key public services by the time of the next election - which is unlikely - they will remain the key issues at that election too.

On these key issues, however, the Conservative Party languishes in public esteem. We are a poor second place to Labour on health and education and in a narrow second place on crime.

Perception is reality

But we suffer from an even more fundamental problem. The public distrust of politicians as a whole has never been more profound. Most people now think all politicians are the same and all in it for themselves. They distrust the motivation of most MPs. This presents a particular problem for the Opposition because all we have to offer are words and promises. A party in government has the opportunity to demonstrate success in the implementation of its policies. A low unemployment, low inflation and strong growth economy is a highly effective public platform for a Government that has been in power for 8 years or more.

> "Whenever we face a decision over policy, our mindset must be driven by the question: what is in the best interests of Britain"

So the first and overwhelmingly important task that the Conservative Party has to face up to is to restore people's faith in us as politicians. It would be difficult to find a more challenging objective but that doesn't lessen its necessity. It can be done but it requires a revolution in the way we as politicians conduct our business and in the mindset that determines every decision and policy stance we take.

It means we have to be scrupulously honest in our deployment of facts and figures. We must eschew yah-boo behaviour in the House of Commons. We must all of us answer questions directly, without equivocation and avoidance. We should admit it when we are wrong and show some humility and humanity. Our language needs to be moderate. We should support the Government when they are right and defend the Government when policies we support are attacked by vested interests. We should bravely oppose the Government

> "Our language needs to be moderate. We should support the Government when they are right and defend the Government when policies we support are attacked by vested interests"

when they are wrong even if to do so would bring ourselves short term unpopularity. And we should never ever succumb to the temptation of opportunism: voting in the No lobby to defeat a policy we believe to be right, such as the privatization of the National Air Traffic-control Service in the 1997 to 2001 Parliament, or tuition fees in the last, just because Tony Blair faces a rebellion from his left wing and we are seduced into trying to inflict a Parliamentary defeat. Such behaviour by our Party merely confirms us in the eyes of the public as motivated by self and the desire for power rather than what is in the best interests of the country. Why do we think people want "Alan B'Stard" type people as their future government?

Whenever we face a decision over policy, our mindset must be driven by the question: what is in the best interests of Britain? It should not be: how can we use this to attack Labour? Or even: how can we use this to gain votes for the Conservative Party? The question must always be: on the basis of what we believe, will this policy help to improve the government of this country?

Some people argue this is naïve, or that it's just motherhood and apple pie. It is neither. It is practical politics. People simply want honesty in the debate about how this country should be run, just as they want an honest bank, a restaurant that doesn't poison them and products that work. They want to hear a politician on the radio and be able to say: how refreshing, a politician I can believe in. That's what we all have to be every minute of the day, every day and without exception. This is not about back to basics. It's far more important than sexual peccadilloes and free nights at the Ritz. It's about being honest in our approach to policy - policy which determines how £700 billion of public money is spent each year, how our health service is run and how we educate our children and tackle crime.

A revolution in public services

In our approach to the three key public services, we need a further revolution in our thinking. And it really does need to be a revolution because for the past two decades or more our approach to reform has been based on structural changes rather than addressing the root causes of their underperformance.

"Both our education system and health service under-perform and they overwhelmingly represent the public's chief concerns"

In education the concept of local management of schools (LMS), where schools receive funding on the basis of the number of pupils, was meant to encourage under-achieving schools to reform themselves and raise standards to the level of the more

Talking About a Revolution

popular schools. But it was the other reforms of the late 1980s that will have had more long term benefits, particularly the introduction of testing at 7, 11 and 14 and the new schools' inspection regime that have enabled us to understand the severity of the problems in our schools.

Yet, today, both our education system and health service under-perform and they overwhelmingly represent the public's chief concerns. Conservative policy at the last election was based on the same approach - choice. By giving parents and patients increased choice, the theory goes, schools and hospitals have to compete for their patronage or fail to receive funding and thus will be forced to provide an efficient and responsive service. So, there is no need for ministers to concern themselves with tackling problems with these services, these will all be taken care of as head teachers and hospital chief executives rush to reform to attract the most discerning parents and patients.

> "Local education authority advisers have far more influence over the state education system than the person the public think is in charge of education - the Secretary of State - who has very little real executive power over the education system"

The problem with this theory, however, is that schools and hospitals within the state sector cannot, in reality, go bust. Nor do they have shareholders willing to sack poor performing management teams. So, unpopular schools limp on with falling rolls and fewer teachers but with thousands of school children condemned to a third rate education.

The drive behind this approach to policy – as with the latest structural proposal, that of localism – is to find a mechanism that implements reform without ministers having to be more involved than passing legislation to implement the new structure. It is part of the trend we have seen over the last few decades of ministers becoming more akin to non-executive directors than chief executives, with executive power vesting increasingly with experts further down the line. This trend is, in part, a consequence of the fall in confidence that politicians feel as trust in them by the public declines. The irony, of course, is that it is the failure of politicians to deliver reform in the public services that is a major factor behind the loss of trust in politicians.

In a democracy the people who run services provided by the state sector should be elected. The private sector is accountable for its performance to the market place. The state sector

> "Thus the three most criticised public services are the ones where accountability is, at best, obscure."

is accountable, in theory, to the electorate. But, over the years, chief constables, schools and hospitals have in practice become less and less accountable to politicians, national or local and less accountable, therefore, to the public.

Chief constables are accountable to a police committee made up of local councillors but even this committee has no jurisdiction over any matters that can be construed as "operational" and they find it very difficult to challenge the authority of the chief constables. Schools are accountable to a partly elected (by a narrow electorate) board of governors and so schools are not accountable either to the local authority or Parliament except indirectly through funding. Hospitals are run by trusts, of which there are about 600 (300 PCTs and 300 hospital trusts), each with its own board of executive and non-executive directors.

Thus the three most criticised public services are the ones where accountability is, at best, obscure.

We need politicians to be far more engaged in understanding why these public services are underperforming. Politicians must take responsibility for ensuring that the public services actually deliver what the public want and should be far more active in defining not only what public services should deliver but how they should be delivered.

The public, for example, want more police patrolling our streets and so the manifestos of all three parties at the last four general elections (1992, 1997, 2001 and 2005) have each promised more police on the beat. Yet over that period we have seen no significant increase in the police presence in our neighbourhoods. And this is principally because most chief constables profoundly disagree with the policy. Politicians, therefore, should be engaged with the Association of Chief Police Officers (ACPO) in debating this very issue rather than supinely allowing the chief constables' view to prevail.

Education standards continue to decline despite claims to the contrary by every Education Secretary. Employers, universities and international studies provide ample evidence for this. One in five 11 year olds leaves primary school unable to read properly. Nearly 40% of 11 year olds cannot write properly. Employers complain of a lack of basic skills amongst school leavers. 23 % of adults cannot read the dosage on an asprin bottle compared to 7% in Sweden and 10% in the Netherlands.

> "The principal problem with the NHS is its appalling management: billions of pounds of waste and inefficiency"

Talking About a Revolution

Yet despite this, politicians have steered clear of the debate about how and what is taught in our schools. Few secondary schools, for example, teach the three sciences as separate subjects at GCSE; only 40% of lessons in comprehensive schools are setted or streamed. There is no requirement for primary schools to teach multiplication tables by rote and so many do not. Why has this approach to education policy been allowed to drift into place with little comment or debate by politicians?

Local education authority advisers have far more influence over the state education system than the person the pubic think is in charge of education – the Secretary of State – who has very little real executive power over the education system. This is why the Government is forced to rely on targets, guidelines, and inspectorates to try to exert influence. This blunt management tool distorts and damages. Targets have resulted in a reduction in exam standards and teachers at primary level "teaching to the test".

The principal problem with the NHS is its appalling management: billions of pounds of waste and inefficiency, MRSA, cancelled operations, lost medical notes, interminable meetings and a culture of malaise that tarnishes the professional excellence of our doctors and nurses. The byzantine structure of its management has made this inevitable, compounded by a powerless Secretary of State attempting to force up standards through the only levers he or she have, that of targets, guidelines and inspectorates, which, as with education, are distorting and fail to tackle the root causes of the problem.

What is needed in health is for politicians to establish clear objectives for hospitals and GP clinics and to establish modern management methods - tried and tested in large private sector organisations throughout the world – to ensure these objectives are delivered. Hospital building programmes, IT systems etc should all be managed nationally. Pay levels, conditions of service should be determined by the local management. We need to see more clinicians taking on senior management roles in the NHS.

> "What is needed in health is for politicians to establish clear objectives... tried and tested in large private sector organisations throughout the world"

This approach to policy is all about the Conservative Party accepting that health and education are in the state sector. It is about eschewing policy that attempts to absolve politicians from the responsibility for reform. It is about the Conservative Party engaging in the issues that go to the root of the problems with our health service, education system and policing. These are the issues that the electorate talk about constantly and that we should too instead of obsessing about structural and electoral changes that make us appear out of touch and ideological.

> "This approach to policy is all about the Conservative Party accepting that health and education are in the state sector"

If we combine a serious approach to the reform of public services, making this our prime concern and campaigning issue, with a new more honest approach to the conduct of politics, we will have a winning formula that will not only win us support but which will also, more importantly, make us highly effective in government.

Politics without a moral purpose is an arid exercise increasingly inappropriate to our age. The time has come for the Conservative Party to recognise that central to its revival and fitness for government should be the embrace of an ethical foreign policy.

Michael Gove MP

Michael was born in 1967 and has been the Member of Parliament for Surrey Heath since May 2005.

Born in Aberdeen and educated at Oxford, where he was President of the Oxford Union, Michael Gove has extensive experience as a journalist and political commentator. He is a regular columnist with *The Times*, having been Editor of *The Saturday Times* and has appeared regularly as a panelist on Radio Four's "The Moral Maze" and BBC Two's "Newsnight Review".

He wrote a biography of Michael Portillo in 1995 and was Chairman of Policy Exchange, a think tank he helped found. He is married to Sarah Vine, who is a leader writer at *The Times*. They have a daughter and a son.

It's Foreign Policy, Stupid...

It isn't just in the American Constitution that certain truths are held to be self-evident. There are certain truths about British politics which are supposed to enjoy the status of unimpeachable wisdom. We are told that oppositions don't win elections, governments lose them, that foreign policy doesn't win elections and politicians who talk about morality set British teeth on edge.

I profoundly disagree with all three judgements. I believe that successful Oppositions, which change how they are seen by the voters, can change the electoral landscape. I think that foreign policy is central to how political organisations are now seen. And I am convinced that politics without a moral purpose is an arid exercise increasingly inappropriate to our age. Which is why I believe that the time has come for Conservatives to recognise that central to our revival, and fitness for government, should be the embrace of an ethical foreign policy.

"The idea that elections are decided by Government success or failure was finally exploded by the 2005 result."

Oppositions can win elections

Let's take each of the three traditional propositions about British politics in turn and see how limited and out of date they are. The idea that elections are decided by government success or failure was finally exploded by the 2005 result. There was widespread dissatisfaction with Labour's performance, specifically its failure to improve public services, and the Prime Minister's own ratings, especially on trust, were pitiably low. Dissatisfaction with the Government was consistently expressed by something close to two thirds of the electorate, and the Government received the lowest share of the vote of any administration for eighty years. But Labour still managed to beat the Conservatives comfortably because, however poorly it performed in popularity tests the Opposition was still considered a less palatable option. Polling by Populus for *The Times* consistently showed that while voters had lost faith in Labour they believed the Conservatives had not done enough to encourage a favourable re-assessment. The lesson was clear. The Conservatives lost the election which it was in the power of an opposition to win because they had not changed sufficiently to

"Polling consistently showed that while voters had lost faith in Labour they believed the Conservatives had not done enough to encourage a favourable re-assessment"

It's Foreign Policy, Stupid...

become an attractive alternative government.

Those who argue that Conservative recovery depends on hitting Labour harder, opposing more vigorously, knocking spots off Blair, tearing into Brown or in some other way further discrediting the Government miss the point. Labour is already unpopular. Our problem is that we are even less liked. Instead of expending energy seeking to further lower Labour in the voters' eyes we need to apply ourselves to elevating our position in the view of our fellow citizens. Oppositions certainly have a limited capacity to influence events, but the one thing we do have the power to change is our own party, how we're seen and the values we promote. Given how poorly we're perceived at the moment the case for change couldn't be stronger.

Changing how the Conservative party operates, and is seen, will involve transforming our approach to a range of issues and adopting a style of politics more in tune with our times. In this essay there is no space to cover every area where we might reform our way of operating but I want to concentrate on one, often seen as marginal to how opposition parties are perceived.

> "Instead of expending energy seeking to further lower Labour in the voters eyes we need to apply ourselves to elevating our position in the view of our fellow citizens"

It's foreign policy, stupid

Foreign affairs have generally been considered peripheral to electoral decision-making. What happens abroad isn't assumed to shift many votes. Certainly, the salience of foreign affairs in pollsters' lists of the issues which decide voting patterns appears to be stubbornly low. But I believe that dramatically understates the growing importance of politicians' attitudes towards global issues in people's judgement of their character, and fitness for office.

Foreign affairs has often, in the past, been viewed as an elite activity, the preserve of a privileged caste of diplomats and statesmen. The personalities of successive Foreign Secretaries, the background of our diplomatic corps, the mystique attaching to foreign affairs think tanks, playing by 'Chatham House' rules, and the apparent detachment of global issues from everyday quality of life

> "Foreign affairs have generally been considered peripheral to electoral decision-making. What happens abroad isn't assumed to shift many votes"

and cost of living policies have reinforced that perception.

Michael Gove

There has, however, always been something inherently flawed in that view. Throughout our history politicians' attitudes to foreign affairs have had a decisive effect on how they have been seen by their contemporaries. At the beginning of the 18th century, the response of rival leaders to the War of the Spanish Succession decisively influenced how the voters judged them. In the 19th century Canning, Palmerston, Gladstone, Disraeli and Salisbury rose and fell through their handling of issues such as the Crimean War, revolution in Continental Europe, repression in the Balkans and conflict in South Africa. In the 20th century the fate, and reputation, of politicians from Lloyd George to Baldwin, Eden to Thatcher, have rested on their handling of foreign affairs.

It shouldn't surprise us. How a politician handles the nation's relations with the rest of the world is decisively revealing of their character, judgement, priorities and vision of the country. Through foreign affairs we can see how political leaders and parties weigh considerations of justice and principle. And that is becoming more important as public engagement with foreign policy deepens.

"Increasingly, the division between foreign and domestic issues is dissolving as citizens see the interconnection between policies"

One of the key trends of our times is the growing, and deepening, popular interest in global issues. On our campuses the issues which move students tend to be foreign policy matters, whether it's the fate of Africa or peace in the Middle East. Among churchgoers political awareness of our global responsibilties is particularly acute and interest in trade, aid and development issues is growing. That interest is becoming ever more widely shared. The success of the Make Poverty History and Trade Justice campaigns, even without the impact of the Live8 concerts, would have marked a shift in public consciouness.

Increasingly political leaders are judged by how they respond to these global challenges. And increasingly, the division between foreign and domestic issues is dissolving as citizens see the interconnection between policies. Agricultural protection at home influences the pace of development in Africa. Instability in central Asia or Latin America influences drug flows onto our streets. Conflict in the Balkans or East Africa drives the migratory patterns which reshape Europe's population. Most powerfully of all, the turbulence within Islam and the nature of Middle Eastern regimes has a direct impact on our security at home.

Voters expect those politicians who aspire to govern Britain to have thought-through responses to these issues. How leaders react to, and seek to shape, these currents gives us an indication of their values and vision. A series of ad hoc, or managerialist, responses will communicate a poverty of vision inadequate to the interconnected challenges of our times.

One of the problems the British Conservatives have had in the recent past is our failure to provide a coherent, narrative for our foreign policy responses. Individual policies towards the crisis in Zimbabwe, the position of Gibraltar and the conflict in Iraq have had much to recommend them, but there has been no linking spine of clearly-enunciated principle behind them. We have looked opportunistic, and in the absence of a modernised account of our actions we have laid ourselves open to caricature as a party whose foreign policy concerns are shaped more by old colonial sentiments than 21st - century realities.

Politicians who have been successful in the past in winning support, and shaping the future, have had a coherent global outlook. Most notably, most recently, Margaret Thatcher's commitment to the spread of liberty on the world stage was integral to the strength of character she communicated.

The need to develop a properly modern Conservative response to the global challenges of our times, as part of a process of proving that we are ready for the responsibilities of government, brings me to my third area of contention. The role of morality.

It has been the traditional view of Conservatives that morals, ethics, highfalutin appeals to values and pious declarations should have no place in foreign affairs, where brute force and *machtpolitik* decide matters between states.

I certainly would never deny the vital importance of force in international relations. One of the reasons why I am a Conservative, and why I believe the Right has a distinctive and valuable advantage in conducting foreign affairs, is our knowledge that the conduct of international relations should not be blinded by idealism about the motives of others. Success in foreign affairs depends on strength, both military and economic, as well as awareness of the self-interest, cynicism and ruthlessness with which other, notably non-democratic, leaders conduct themselves.

"Success in foreign affairs depends on strength, both military and economic, as well as awareness of the self-interest, cynicism and ruthlessness with which other, notably non-democratic leaders conduct themselves"

But knowledge that other actors are operating amorally does not absolve us of the need to have a moral dimension to our policies. Quite the opposite.

Foreign affairs will often require national leaders to take risks, assume positions and expend resources which, in a modern democracy, will require popular support. The age, if it ever existed, when leaders could adopt diplomatic positions and escape democratic scrutiny of their actions, is gone. If difficult decisions are to be taken and, more importantly, if policies are to be maintained over the period necessary to secure results then there needs to be a broad understanding of the principled motivation underlying actions. Only by explaining, and justifying, the vision which guides action can democratic assent be secured over time. And in our age, it is increasingly difficult to secure democratic support without a proper articulation of the moral case for action. One of the reasons why the Blair Government has run into difficulties with domestic opinion over Iraq has been the administration's failure to make the moral case for its actions sufficiently early, sufficiently clearly and sufficiently often. By rooting the case for intervention on the narrow grounds of the WMD threat Mr Blair was true neither to himself nor the importance of the war, and he has suffered for that.

There is another reason why foreign affairs needs to be infused with a moral dimension. The sheer affront to human decency of the scale of global suffering. With so many denied food, dignity, liberty and the chance to lead proper lives free of fear there is a pressing need for global action. Compassion doesn't stop at our borders and, as we know they are increasingly porous and our world is ever more interconnected.

During the Cold War the threat from communism, and related security considerations, impeded our ability to use our power for good across the globe. Defeating an ideology which has been responsible for more human suffering than any other belief system was both a matter of national self-interest and moral urgency. Now, in a world where the West has greater, although still limited, freedom to act, we can do more to alleviate suffering, extend liberty, and defend civilized values. Political leaders who duck this challenge will deserve the hostility of voters and a grim verdict from posterity.

"In the past Conservatives have often acquiesced in support for sordid regimes on the basis that they provided stability in strategic regions. But our support for these regimes has been progressively counter-productive"

Of course, the scope for idealism in foreign policy is necessarily

It's Foreign Policy, Stupid...

constrained at the moment by the security challenges we still face, not least from Islamist terrorism and rising Chinese power. But against both these dangers morality is a vital strategic asset, not an impediment to action. As we found during the Cold War, our strongest allies against totalitarian enemies were the people they oppressed. The strength, and promise, of democracy gave hope to those suffering under Soviet communism just as it gives hope to the oppressed from Tehran to Beijing.

In the past Conservatives have often acquiesced in support for sordid regimes on the basis that they provided 'stability', secure trading partners and military support in strategic regions. But our support for these regimes has been increasingly counter-productive. In the Middle East, those repressive regimes we support, such as Egypt and Saudi Arabia, have been incubators of terror whose population is resentfully, and understandably, anti-Western. But in those countries where we have opposed the oppressors, such as Iran, the West enjoys mass popular support and the democratic dynamic is in our favour. Support for democratisation is not just the moral course in foreign policy, it also the only prudential way to proceed. It is the alternative, realpolitik, path which has contributed to the current terrorist threat.

A Conservative Party which articulated the case for an ethical foreign policy, rooted in a vision of global justice, driven by a passion for human rights and determined to defend the cause of liberty would transform itself in the eyes of the voters into a truly modern alternative government. And that, vitally, would give our generation the chance to transform our world for the better.

A sustainable approach to running the economy which incentivises our society, a country where our law counts and is enforced, and education and healthcare that match up to what we need and the tax we pay.

Justine Greening MP

Justine Greening was born in 1969 and captured Putney, David Mellor's old seat, in the 2005 General Election with a slender majority of 1766. Born in Rotherham, South Yorkshire, she was educated at Southampton University and has a Masters degree from the London Business School.

Formerly the Bow Group's Political Officer, she is an accountant by training and has worked for PricewaterhouseCoopers, SmithKline Beecham, and Centrica. She has served on Epping Council, and is focused on the community and women in politics.

A Winning Formula

I've only been an MP for just over two months, but there's no doubt that whether you're inside or outside of Westminster, the question of how to get victory at the next election has had more than its fair share of discussion and debating time. Everyone has their view – brand, campaigning, fighting off the Lib Dems – pet theories constantly abound.

Having spent 15 years in business before entering Parliament earlier this year, whenever apparently insoluble questions arise, I tend to equate any situation with one that I might come across in business and ask myself how I'd deal with it. It's surprising how obvious the answers are that emerge.

"What the Conservative Party needs to do - work out what the key factors were in winning the seats we actually won back from Labour and those that we just missed out on but had hefty swings in"

So, to analogise our Party's situation to one in business: if you were the board director of a company who had had static sales for several years but needed to get a nationwide rise in sales, what would you do? Look for facts and data, for a start – where are sales going badly and where are they going well? When you reviewed the Conservative Party 'sales by area' analysis, you'd very quickly see that in some pilot areas, product sales had actually done pretty well. Sales had risen, and customers had switched to buying your product.

Any board director with half a brain would then want to find out what happened in those areas were sales had gone well to see if there were particular factors that could be applied nationwide.

"A general election is won or lost in the years before the campaign - if you're behind at the start of the election campaign, it's hard to overtake on the home stretch"

That's what the Conservative Party needs to do: work out what the key factors were in winning the seats we actually won back from Labour and those that we just missed out on but had hefty swings in. When you do this, a few things become very clear.

Fighting an effective campaign

A general election is won or lost in the years before the campaign, less so in the election itself – if you're behind at the start of the election, it's very hard to overtake on the home stretch. For almost

79

A Winning Formula

all successful target seat candidates (now MPs), the election was the culmination of three years of hard work, often longer – the election was icing on a cake that had been carefully baked over many, many months. That suggests that the Conservative Party is correct to get a new leader early in this Parliament who can get stuck into the job and get some traction with the electorate.

Candidates who won back constituencies tended to focus very strongly on local issues, plugging away on them over many years. They took residents' issues and made them their own. My agenda in Putney was set not by myself as candidate, but by my fellow residents – I fought over the months and years as candidate on the issues they told me mattered to them most. I took the actions and made the case I would have done if I had already been MP – I tried to 'out-MP' the previous MP. If the issue was excessive aircraft noise from planes landing very early the morning, I worked out what needed to be done to solve the issue – often several pieces of effort – and then took those actions. My leaflets told people not what I thought about issues, but what I'd done.

> "My agenda in Putney was set not by myself as candidate, but by my fellow residents – I fought over the months and years as candidate on the issues they told me mattered to them most"

That has some important implications for us. If we applied that thinking to the national party, it suggests that our political agenda needs to be quite simply taking the country's priorities and making them our own. Our agenda has to be centred around what matters to our country and its people most. We need to own those issues in the minds of voters by speaking out on them regularly, urging for action on them or even best taking direct action ourselves as an opposition if that's possible.

I spent three years working away on the same four major issues in Putney. In spite of my consistency, it took all of that time before people got to remember that I campaigned on crime, aircraft noise, the District Line tube and postal services. It shows how often a message needs to be repeated before it will truly register with voters. And why not – we all get bombarded with facts and leaflets every day. Why should I remember Conservative Party priorities any more than I remember McDonald's latest product launch - and they have TV adverts telling us about their products every day. Whenever we appear to a mass audience we need to have the same message. It will eventually percolate through into people's minds.

All of that implies being clear cut on fighting for our country's priorities well in advance of the election. Because we have a government that is shameless in using our ideas to its advantage, this poses some challenges. However, that is a risk we will have to take. We have to believe that people will respect us for being clear cut, for being up front with them about what voting Conservative means. And we might just be better placed to starting winning the odd by-election…

> "I spent three years working away on the same four major issues in Putney… it shows how often a message needs to be repeated before it will truly register with voters"

Campaigning priorities

So, we have some potential ingredients for success, but what are these priorities for the country priorities that we should make our own? Well, I'll have a stab at that too based on my significant door-knocking over three years in Putney, talking with thousands of residents there, and the resultant sense of what needs sorting out.

The economy. Gordon Brown is not running the economy in a sustainable way and that puts us all in economic peril. We cannot forever build up national and personal debt as we are doing right now. That proposal suggests a much broader argument for us as a party than just tax – rather our argument needs to be about balancing the books more sensibly, taxing and spending affordably. We need to argue for an economy that works with the grain of human nature, not against it, i.e. effort and reward are closely linked. Coming out of that would be policies that emphasised savings, potentially root and branch reform of the tax, benefit, and tax credits system as a whole not separately, pension reform centre stage and challenged means testing (and I'll make a suggestion that we need to specifically address the issue of womens' pensions) – and interestingly whilst we're on debt and saving, tuition fees. For me a university degree was the key to financial independence but what about today? Is it wise to have so many twenty somethings with so much debt, dependent on a buoyant economy?

> "Gordon Brown is not running the economy in a sustainable way and that puts us all in economic peril."

Crime. I never remember anyone agreeing that not all of this country's laws should be enforced. All of them should. It's a matter of principle and of ensuring that we feel secure in our

81

homes and communities. Too much of the criminal activity in our country goes unchallenged, so I'd like to see a series of actions well beyond just having more police. We need to ensure our courts can cope, our prisons can cope and that we tackle head on the root cause of so much crime – drug addiction. Education and rehab places – we need to do what it takes to extinguish demand.

Public services. The vast majority of the people in this country are reliant for their health and education on the state and have paid up front for them with taxes. We have to build a plan for those public services that will truly tackle today's issues of challenged standards and poor choice. In this area, I believe we have moved in the right direction as a party, but there is more to be done. Perhaps here we have the biggest challenge. As a nation we have some difficult questions to answer. Our Conservative Party should have the courage to start the debate in way that people can engage in it with us.

That's the main agenda I believe the country needs us to have – a sustainable approach to running the economy which incentivises our society, a country where our law counts and is enforced, and education and healthcare that match up to what we need and the tax we pay. It's not exclusive – I might be tempted to add environment too. But, if we can't win on the main agenda with voters, we won't win at all.

If the Conservatives can fundamentally change their message and narrative so that it is based first and foremost on social justice, on aspiration and merit then there is real chance that we Conservatives will reconnect with the people of Britain once again.

Robert Halfon
Conservative Parliamentary Candidate for Harlow 2005

Robert Halfon has been involved in the Conservative Party for 22 years. He is a former Chief of Staff to Rt Hon Oliver Letwin MP and was a Director of the Renewing One Nation Think Tank founded by Lord Kalms and William Hague in 2000. Robert is a Board Member of the Centre for Social Justice, established by Iain Duncan Smith in 2004. He is currently Political Director of Conservative Friends of Israel and acts as a political adviser to a number of right of centre organisations. He is the author of numerous articles and a number of pamphlets on Conservatism as well as subjects as diverse as Russia and Corporate Responsibility. In 2001, Robert fought Harlow and cut Labour's majority from 10,514 to 5,200 with a 4.5% swing. Standing for the constituency again in 2005, Labour's majority was reduced from 5,228 to just 97 with a swing of 6.4% and an increase in vote share of 6.4%.

A Just Society

Harlow constituency should be Conservative held. The fact that after two elections, Labour hold it now by a majority of just 97 votes (down from 10,500 in 1997), should not be a cause of congratulation but rather a symbol of our collective failure as a Party to connect with the people of Britain over the past two elections.

Labour's majority was cut in Harlow (the Conservative vote share increased by 6.4%) thanks to the superhuman efforts of dedicated volunteers over many years. But, however successful we were organisationally, it is incredibly difficult to buck the national trend. Unless we as a Party nationally really begin to connect with voters at a personal and local level, the chances are that we will face huge obstacles to winning Harlow and other similar constituencies at the next election.

A new town surrounded by picturesque villages and beautiful countryside, Harlow has strong Conservative roots. Winston Churchill represented Harlow, when the area came under Epping, as did Norman Tebbit during the 1970s. After boundary changes, Harlow voted Labour only to return to the Conservative fold in 1983.

"The general view was that Conservatives represented privilege, were too caught up in the Westminster village, and had no plausible answers to the everyday failures in public services"

Throughout the 1980s, attracted by Conservative aspirational policies of lower taxes and home ownership (the right to buy), Harlow consistently returned a Conservative MP (Jerry Hayes), until the Tory disaster of the 1997 election.

Disconnected from voters

So why have Conservatives failed in seats like Harlow? Of course there are local and national organisational improvements that could make a difference. But the reasons for failure are much deeper.

Having fought Harlow twice as a Parliamentary Candidate, five negatives came up time and time again on the doorstep:

- The Conservatives do not stand for anything (or what does it mean to be a Conservative?).

- The Conservatives do not reflect our aspirations.

- The Conservatives are opportunistic.

- The Conservatives are the party of toffs and care little about the poor.
- The Conservatives speak in a language that we don't understand.

Underlying all these things was a real perception that the Conservatives did not know what it was like for individuals and families to struggle to keep their head above water and enjoy a decent standard of living.

During the election a mother approached me saying that she worked nights and her husband worked days in order to ensure that their children had a good life. She thought that the Conservatives had offered nothing to families similar to hers. This lady's message was simple: she or her husband would not vote Conservative again, until Conservatives stood up for hard working individuals who had to work too hard in order to earn a living and have some quality of life.

The general view was that Conservatives represented privilege, were too caught up in the Westminster village, and had no plausible answers to the everyday failures in public services.

Of course many of them had heard the ten word mantra, but few understood or were convinced about the detailed policies that came behind them. 'Choice' and the ten words came to be seen as just that – 'words', things that that every politician from every party promised.

In addition people were convinced by Labour scare tactics over the economy. Despite over a decade after ERM, there were many who were scarred by the high interest rates, bankruptcies and recession of that time.

Winning again

The strangest thing about being a Conservative is that there are many people who share conservative views but would not think of voting Conservative. At the heart of this problem lies a belief that Conservatives are exclusive, care nothing for the poor and know nothing about real life.

> "The strangest thing about being a Conservative is that there are many people who share conservative views but would not think of voting Conservative"

Of course the opposite is true. Thousands of dedicated party activists not only come from modest backgrounds but dedicate their life to volunteering and charitable endeavours. Yet perception is everything, and – in an age of media manipulation – it can often overtake reality.

Nevertheless, despite these perceptions. there are grounds for optimism. When new Labour was in opposition, Tony Blair saw it as the party's main goal to change a number of negative perceptions about itself. Mr Blair turned all the negatives about Labour into advantages. The most notable of course was that 'new' Labour could look after the economy well and would be tough on crime. Similarly, through its actions and its narrative, the Conservatives can change perceptions as to how people view the Party.

So what can the Conservatives do? What is the political agenda that will return seats like Harlow, Crawley, and Sittingbourne to the Conservative fold (all seats with a Labour majority of less than 100)?

First the Conservative Party needs to ensure that it is seen as transparent and open by the British public. It also needs to act and behave in a way which is demonstrably unlike what we currently know as a traditional Westminster party.

Second, the Conservative Party should develop a simple narrative around social justice and compassion. These should act as the glue that binds all the policies together.

Transparency and openness

The Conservatives should break out of the Westminster village. Conservatives need to be seen and heard across the country. The new politics is crying out for a change. It is often said that people are fed up with politics hence the low voter turnout. The reality is that they are fed up with political parties not politics. That is why membership of all the major parties has fallen whilst that of pressure groups has risen. For a political party to succeed it therefore needs to behave more like a successful pressure group: open, transparent, power given to individual members and having a simple narrative and message.

Every weekly Shadow Cabinet meeting should be held in a different area of Britain and wherever that Shadow meeting is to be held, there should be a day's campaigning. Senior Shadow Ministers who are not in the Shadow Cabinet should be tasked with managing the majority of Parliamentary affairs. The Shadow Cabinet should spend most of their time outside Westminster.

Backbench MPs, especially the newly elected Members, should be responsible for adopting constituencies that have little Conservative representation (e.g. places like Islington, constituencies in Scotland and Liverpool, Manchester and Birmingham). The MPs should be responsible for building up the membership in these areas and trying to ensure local council representation. Not only will this help build a truly mass membership party, but will also ensure that Conservatives are not exclusively influenced by rural areas of Britain or the South East.

> "For a political party to succeed it therefore needs to behave more like a successful pressure group: open, transparent, power given to individual members and having a simple narrative and message"

It is a frightening thought that so many areas in the country have not had any real Conservative activity for years. There should be no no-go areas for the Conservative Party. Never again should we describe areas where we lose by-elections as 'left-wing territory' or 'not natural territory'.

Independent MPs

Conservatives also need a revolution in Parliament. At present most of the electorate see MPs from the main parties as being placemen and yes men and the like. There is a deep yearning for independence of spirit and conviction politics.

> "Never again should we describe areas where we lose by-elections as 'left-wing territory' or 'not natural territory'"

A new Leader should announce that the Conservative Whip should be relaxed for most votes – except for front bench MPs. This will allow MPs to vote according to conscience. Of course the media would try to highlight divisions, but if this was announced as a conscious policy from the beginning, Conservatives would give a clear illustration to the electorate that they were different to the usual run of politicians. It would allow MPs to truly serve the constituents rather than just being placemen of the party Whips. What better example could there be of honest politics and a changing Conservative Party?

A mass membership party

The Conservatives should not duck the challenge of creating a mass membership party. The recent moves to curtail party members from having a real say in the leadership election will hinder this as people who join organisations want real involvement in decision making and not just to be sent a newsletter once a month. As Theresa May MP has argued, to create a mass membership party, the Conservatives need to be innovative and forward looking, and introduce an electoral college and primaries for the election of a leader. Similarly Parliamentary Candidates could be chosen via the same method. If people have moved towards activist pressure group politics, then the Conservative Party needs to do the same.

Social justice

The terms 'compassion' or 'social justice' are sometimes viewed with suspicion by those of a Conservative disposition. Underlying this is a view that it represents a kind of Conservatism that seeks a bigger role for the state and increased public spending.

In fact the opposite is the case. Social justice is about fighting privilege and promoting aspiration and merit. It is about ensuring that everyone has access to the best public services not just the pushy or the well off. It means cascading wealth down to the poorest through the tax system. It encourages the social entrepreneurialism of community - minded individuals, as they seek to transform their neighbourhoods. It makes certain that the liberty of individuals, families and communities are protected and not constrained by a controlling government. It supports a foreign policy of idealism without illusions and concentrates on international development and stopping mass genocide.

> "Imagine if Conservatives announced that social justice would be the main principle that all its policies were to be built on... Over time, Conservatives would lose the tag of being seen as the party of privilege."

Imagine if Conservatives announced that social justice would be the main principle that all its policies were to be built on. Imagine if every speech, every press release, every announcement, every party broadcast reflected the social justice agenda. Imagine too, if the new leader and members of the Shadow Cabinet went out on a regular basis to the poorest areas of Britain to seek ways of improving the lives of those most in need.

If it was done properly, without cynicism, and sustained over the next four years, the effect of the perception of the Party could be enormous. Over time, Conservatives would lose the tag of being seen as the party of privilege. It would weaken Labour's false claim to be the party of the poor. Not only would the Conservatives be offering something for the many forgotten people across the council estates of Britain, but we would convince the many floating voters that voting Conservative is not just about self interest, but a noble and moral thing to do.

But, this will only work if – in contrast to the previous brave 'help the vulnerable campaign' during the leadership of Iain Duncan Smith – a new social justice campaign would have the support of the whole front bench and the Party at large behind it. It would only succeed if the social justice agenda were not blown off course by short - term pressures to place 'core vote' stories in the tabloids.

A Just Society

Four immediate steps to further the social justice agenda

- The new leader should appoint at Shadow Cabinet level, a Shadow Minister whose sole role is to promote social justice and co-ordinate across overlapping departments. In order for this Shadow Cabinet Minister to have teeth, he or she should have to report to the leader on a weekly basis as to progress.

- The new leader should announce that the Shadow Cabinet will begin an investigation of the worst 100 council estates in Britain and report their findings to the Party Conference in 2006. This investigation would be carried out by MPs and activists who would each be tasked with an individual council estate and canvassing the views of residents.

- Parliamentary Candidates should be tasked with pursuing the social justice agenda in their own constituencies reporting back to the Shadow Cabinet Minister. Conservative Council group leaders should have as a major responsibility to further the social justice agenda in individual wards. Candidates and councillors who make major strides towards achieving the social justice agenda should be rewarded by special targeting and financial assistance from Conservative Central Office.

- The Centre for Social Justice, the think tank established by Iain Duncan Smith MP, should be attached to the leader's policy unit and given the task of developing policies on social justice in time for the Manifesto and sent round the country to speak to Conservative Associations/clubs/committees about furthering the social justice agenda.

A vision for the future

If the Conservatives can fundamentally change their message and narrative so that it is based first and foremost on social justice, on aspiration and merit, then there is a real chance that we Conservatives will reconnect with the people of Britain once again. If we can show the voters that we do understand the daily struggle and fears that many voters have to face in their daily lives, there is a chance that people will start believing that we can make a difference.

But none of this will happen unless the Conservatives really break out of the Westminster village and are constantly amongst the people they hope to represent. If Conservatives speak out of principle and not opportunism, if they adopt honest politics at all times, if they positively allow and encourage open debate amongst backbench MPs, Parliamentary Candidates and councillors, if joining the Conservative Party means real decision making and real involvement, then there is every chance that instead of saying Harlow should be a Conservative constituency, that Harlow is now Conservative held.

The public suspected our motives because they did not understand our vision. New Labour have stolen our policies and effectively hijacked the centre right agenda so that the Tory party is seen as extreme and out of touch.

Andrew Lansley CBE MP
Shadow Secretary of State for Health

Andrew Lansley was born in 1956 and has been the Member of Parliament for South Cambridgeshire since 1997. Andrew is the Shadow Secretary of State for Health and has served on the Health Select Committee and as Secretary of the Backbench Trade and Industry Committee and the Environment, Transport and Regions Backbench Committee.

Andrew was educated at Essex University where he was President of the Guild of Students. Prior to politics he was a civil servant (he was Principal Private Secretary to Lord Tebbit) from 1979 to 1984, after which he was Director of the Conservative Research Department. He is married to Sally and has four daughters and a son.

Power of Positive Politics

Elections are won and lost over four years. The most significant point Michael Howard made in his remarks in Putney, the day after the General Election, was that he wanted his successor to have the time he didn't have.

For all our tactical successes, the last Parliament was a strategic failure.

The strategic failure of the 2005 general election

In 1992, the Conservative Party polled 14 million votes. In 2005, we polled 8.8 million votes. Compared to 2001 our vote increased by just 410,000. Labour lost 1.17 million votes. The Liberal Democrats gained 1.17 million. For every vote gained direct from Labour, the Liberal Democrats got two. We only gained ground in London, the South East and East of England. We gained ground amongst working class voters, but lost it among AB voters.

In terms of which party was thought to have the best policies on health and education, Labour's lead over us halved compared to 2001, but on the economy their lead increased.

We increased our support among men, but lost ground among women voters. It is deeply disturbing that our support among women aged 25-54 fell sharply (by 4 percentage points), even while it went up among men of the same ages. If we had secured the same level of support among women as men, Labour would have lost their majority.

> "It is deeply disturbing that our support among women fell sharply. If we had secured the same level of support among men as women, Labour would have lost their majority"

Is it because we are a party of men? Of 54 new Conservative MPs, only 6 are women. Of 197 Conservative MPs, only 17 are women. Of 354 Labour MPs, 97 are women – four times that proportion. If we had secured 354 seats, fewer than 50 would be women.

So when the Conservative Party fails to draw women into its positions of leadership, while the majority of new entrants to some other professions, like medicine and the law, are women, people will ask: do they represent us or understand my problems?

The fact that we announced good flexible childcare proposals late on in the campaign did not offset the fact that we had insufficient policies to support parents in bringing up their children. The

Power of Positive Politics

phrase 'balancing work and family life' makes it sound so simple, but it is about having to make hard, painful decisions on how to maintain family income whilst also being at home and being there for the children. Sally and I know how hard these decisions are; we live with that right now.

When Jamie Oliver captured exactly what millions of parents feel about school food, did they hear us respond?

Where, in our ten words, was the recognition that family is the backbone of a strong society?

And are younger women voters unwilling to support a party which they regard as extreme?

Winning the emotional argument

When Labour was the party regarded as extreme, the Conservative Party was able to lead from the right. With the Labour Party seen as camped on the centre ground of politics, right-wing policies are characterised as extreme.

Of course, the political spectrum doesn't offer centrist solutions to every issue. School choice or competition and choice in health come from centre right philosophy, but are being accepted even by socialists. In Stockholm I heard exactly how that had happened because school vouchers are a success in Sweden. The reason it is not regarded as extreme or ideological is because choice is for everyone regardless of their ability to pay.

> "When Mr. Blair talks of being relentlessly new Labour what he means is occupying more centre-right territory. And he hopes our response will be to push to the right"

What is the centrist view of ID cards? What is the centrist view of whether workplace pension provision should be voluntary or compulsory, opt - in or opt - out? In reality, there are left - of - centre, statist, collectivist solutions, and centre-right market-orientated, decentralised, community-based, deregulated solutions.

When Mr. Blair talks of being "relentlessly new Labour" what he means is occupying more centre-right territory. And he hopes our response will be to push to the right. The result is that a significant proportion of the population regard us as out of line with their view. We cannot afford for this to continue. Mr Blair knows centre-right policies are winning the intellectual argument. We need to win the emotional argument; show that we understand

and that we know how people feel. That what we propose as policies comes from a positive sense of what our country, and every family in it needs.

I expressed much of the same analysis after the 2001 election. I said then that we need to ensure we have a party representative of the public we wish to serve. In 2001, I said that we had learnt a powerful lesson. We can have all the policies we like, even policies the public like, but if the public do not trust us, they will not endorse our policies or give us the credit for them. Labour can steal our policies and get away with it. They do; and they have.

> "We can have all the policies we like, even policies the public like, but if the public do not trust us, they will not endorse our policies or give us the credit for them"

As I put it four years ago, governments are judged by what they do and Opposition are judged for who they are.

Remember: in 1999, the Common Sense Revolution was focussed on health and education – the Patient's Guarantee and Free Schools. In 2002, Iain Duncan Smith made 'helping the vulnerable' and social justice his key emphases. This tells us how tough it is. It's not just policy. It's about the whole Party. It's about real convictions. It must be real. It must be sustained. It must be positive. It must be with a passion.

Freedom for all

The Conservative Party has always changed as Britain and its needs have changed. We don't believe in change for its own sake, but for a purpose.

After 1979 we had passion for change. We had to defeat the power of union barons, restore the value of money and make Britain great again. In the 1980s Margaret Thatcher's Government created a dynamic economy. They defeated communism.

Today we face new major threats: terrorism, climate change, international poverty.

And major challenges: crime, anti-social behaviour and the fear of crime, inadequate standards of health, education and transport, businesses losing competitiveness in international markets.

> "Think of our children. Yes, we do give them their freedom, progressively, and help them to use that freedom to realise their hopes and dreams. But they need far more than that. They need values"

These are the challenges today. We need a passion for change. And I believe that passion has to come from a love of freedom and of family. Freedom is defined negatively by some – leave me alone, don't interfere, get government off my back. But freedom must be positive. Freedom which gives hope, opportunity, prosperity and security. We must recognise that freedom is for everyone. It is freedom from poverty for a child in Tower Hamlets as much as it is freedom two miles away for the businessman in the City of London from excessive regulation.

It is a freedom to live our lives and spend our hard-earned income, for us and our families. It is freedom for enterprise to create wealth. Freedom is essential to delivering sustained economic performance. Free markets, free enterprise and free trade.

And it requires positive action to create other freedoms: freedom from the fear of crime and anti-social behaviour; freedom from poverty; freedom from ignorance; freedom from disease. Giving people access to the freedom that comes with good health, high standards of education and eradicating poverty is a positive philosophy of freedom which we have to articulate. Freedom is not licence. It is not merely the absence of constraint. Positive freedom is about empowerment: it's about a child being able to go to a school which realises their potential; disabled people not being left out of employment; the single parent given support so the child has the right role model and the parent an opportunity to work. It's even about giving millions of children in Africa the basic right to live. If we believe in freedom and give people freedom, we give them hope in the future. Nothing is more important than that.

Yet all of these freedoms are not enough. Freedoms give us hope, and opportunity, but not necessarily security. Think of our children. Yes, we do give them their freedom, progressively, and help them to use that freedom to realise their hopes and dreams. But they need for more than that. They need values. They need to learn. They need to be guided. They need to gain their independence within boundaries. As they gain their freedom, they need to know that they are loved, supported and if need be, protected. They need, in short, family. Family which, in 21st century Britain, takes many forms, but which we all know, is composed of those who love us and care for us.

Mr Blair talks about respect. Where does he think it comes from? Not from a state which nationalises compassion and puts bureaucracy in place of family.

People have come to the Conservative Party for many reasons. I came to the Conservative Party because, under Margaret

Thatcher, I could see that freedom was transforming Britain's economy, bringing us prosperity.

> "The public think freedom for Conservatives means "I'll do as I like and you'll lose out" and respect means "Do as I tell you." When Conservatives talk of family, people remember 'back to basics'"

I decided to enter politics in 1989, I remember the sense of awe and excitement at what our philosophy of freedom could achieve, when representatives of newly-free states of Central and Eastern Europe came to our 1990 Party Conference.

And, as a Conservative, I have found more. Respect for the ties that bind us together, from family to church, to nation. These are real and without them, freedom delivers opportunity, but not compassion and security.

Positive politics

As things stand, the public think freedom for Conservatives means "I'll do as I like and you'll lose out" and respect means "Do as I tell you." When Conservatives talk of family, people remember 'back to basics'. This has to change. Because we have to change.

We have to bring forward a new generation and new representatives for the party. To understand Britain as it is today. To be seen to lead normal lives and to share people's ambitions; where "spending more time with my family" isn't regarded by Westminster politicians as code for a leadership bid. To want to improve people's lives, but through listening, so that we respond to people's hopes. And we must be a party which through its actions secures trust. Trust is vital. Trust is indivisible. You aren't trusted a bit on this and not on that. Only by our actions will we win back trust. And it can only be earned if we are, and are seen to have integrity, to be honest, compassionate, tolerant, generous, realistic, competent, united and loyal to each other.

> "It may lose us the easy 'attack dog' options, but we should be less strident and more interesting"

I know that none of this defines the detail of the policies we should pursue. I know the temptations. I do policy. I believe policy - making is a key skill. I have ideas for how policies must be shaped. Policies which harness technology and free enterprise to the challenge of climate change. Which prioritise free trade and good governance to tackle global poverty. Which through a national framework of standards and funding in health and education enable competition and choice to be combined with genuine equity of access.

Policy which gives parents more viable childcare options and strengthens the family. Which sets local government free. Which reforms and simplifies tax. Which shifts power into the hands of consumers rather than bureaucracy and cuts government budgets in the process. Which reinforces local policing and local communities.

And it is not enough simply to have lots of new policies in different areas – school choice, freedom for hospitals and so on. We had lots of new policies. The problem was that the public suspected our motives because they did not understand our vision. Let me give you an example. When Conservatives talk about school choice, the public imagine it is due to some Conservative obsession with markets, efficiency and productivity. They treat our policy announcements with suspicion. But if we explain first that that we have a positive vision for education, that situation will change. So we need to start by saying that we have a vision for a country where children from all backgrounds have equal and outstanding opportunities. No matter what their background, all children should be given the opportunity to fulfil their full potential. This is not happening under Labour. Under Labour, parents are forced to buy their children a good education by going private or moving to a good catchment area, where house prices are higher. Or else, like I did for my eldest daughter, fight long appeals to get the school of their choice. We must have a vision for the country where this unfairness does not happen. Then we must say that we will make our positive vision a reality through school choice. When voters understand our vision, they will be more likely to accept our policies.

"The problem was that the public suspected our motives because they did not understand our vision"

Policy must come from our values. Who we are, and what we stand for must be established by us, with the people, before we set out what we offer in policy terms. A key step will be to signal our priorities by establishing policy commissions which both develop policy and create long-lasting networks through which future policy can be tested with those directly involved. These should include: a commission on the family; a commission for a strong economy; a commission on climate change; a commission on reform of public services; and a commission on international development.

There will be those who argue that the key to our success is in our effectiveness in opposing Labour, in articulating their failures to deliver, in the aggression we show. I do not underestimate the effectiveness of this. The public and the media hear negative views more easily than positive ones. But negative politics is not the same as opposition. And persuading people not to vote Labour is not the same as convincing them to vote Conservative. As Philip Gould said of Labour prior to 1997, the electorate would not accept negative attacks unless they were balanced by positive messages or themes. A critique of ones' opponents can be deployed without descending to abuse, to personal attacks or opposition for its own sake.

It may lose us the easy 'attack dog' options, but we should be less strident and more interesting.

Not only the positive presentation of conservative priorities and policies is required, but a positive approach to the role of politicians and opposition is integral to the change we have to make.

"We have to encourage Conservative MPs to bring to their Westminster politics the same care and concerns which they exhibit in their constituencies"

More free votes, so that the people's representatives in Parliament make real decisions for themselves. Less obsessive control by the Whips, a recognition of the distinctive role of Parliament, effective scrutiny of expenditures, all of these are part of the positive shift. We have to encourage Conservative MPs to bring to their Westminster politics the same care and concerns which they exhibit in their constituencies. We have to develop our capacity to identify and investigate issues. To think long-term and develop campaigns. To listen to and reflect the concerns of the public. In contact not just with the party faithful, but with the public we have to reach.

To build teams, in Parliament and beyond, who are committed to their issues. Teams which combine a passion for their subject, with proven competence. Teams which ensure that we combine substance with changes in style.

Many of these ideas have been floated before, but it has been just that. Floated in, and floated off. What we have lacked is the coherence, the sustained effort, and the strategic context to see a process of reform through. Just as an election campaign itself requires focus and discipline, so does a strategy. For the Conservative Party to reform itself, to convince the electorate that we can be trusted to reform Britain, to deliver a dynamic economy again, to deliver public service reform, to meet long-term aspirations for our children, to combat poverty and to tackle climate change, will require them to lose deep-seated prejudices against the Conservative Party. It will need us to show we have changed and that we are trustworthy and competent. That we know where we are going. That our positive principles of freedom and family mean hope for the future and positive reassurance that the Conservative Party will enable them to fulfil their aspirations, to lead a better life for them and their families.

The reforms must be phased and they must be clear: immediately to reform the Conservative Party from within; rapidly to reach out on the basis of a positive renewal of our values and principles, to show we share the public's concerns and hopes; and progressively to demonstrate, towards the election, how we will deliver hope for the people of Britain.

In 1979, the Conservatives were faced with the challenge of sorting out a poor economy that was failing a poor country. Today's challenge is to sort out a poor government that is failing a rich country. So long as 'modernising' remains nothing more than being 'less strident in tone', more caring or nicer younger gayer, than the Tories of the '80s, then the Conservative Party will remain dead in the political water.

Rt Hon Theresa May MP
Shadow Secretary of State for the Family and for Culture, Media & Sport

Theresa may was born in 1956 and is the Member of Parliament for Maidenhead where she increased her majority in the 2005 General Election despite a Liberal Democrat decapitation strategy to unseat her. Theresa has been a Shadow Secretary of State since 1999; Education & Employment; Transport, Local Government & the Regions; Transport; Environment & Transport; the Family. The Culture, Media and Sport portfolio was added to her brief after the 2005 General Election. She was Chairman of the Conservative Party from 2002-2003. Educated at Oxford, she worked in the banking industry prior to entering parliament and was Head of European Affairs and an Adviser on International Affairs at the Association of Payment Clearing Services. She is married to Philip and they live in Sonning in Maidenhead.

Reassembling the Jigsaw

The Conservative Party is in uncharted waters. The Party has just suffered a historic third election defeat in a row, with its reward for running an efficient and vigorous campaign being to win just one third of the popular vote: less than Michael Foot's Labour Party received in 1983.

Yet when analysed in greater depth, the results paint an even starker picture. We lost votes in the majority of the country outside the South East and Wales. We lost votes in cities like Manchester, Birmingham and Leeds, where we once had Conservative MPs, but where our vote has in some cases now reduced to a fifth of what it was. And we lost votes amongst young professionals, among the 35 to 54 year olds, and most importantly, among women.

How different things were when we were winning elections under Margaret Thatcher. In 1979, Conservatives held more than a 35% lead amongst middle class AB1 voters and this lead increased to almost 40% in 1983. By 2005, our lead among AB1s was statistically insignificant.

Arguably even more important has been the loss of the women's vote, and the abandonment of the Tory brand by 'Worcester woman'. The Conservative Party won more than 40% of the women's vote in all the elections from 1979 to 1992, and consequently won all those elections. We used to be the party of the woman voter – the housewives' choice – and every election we have won since the war has been on the basis of a majority of the female vote. In 2005, we managed to secure the support of just 32% of women who voted.

> "We used to be the party of the woman voter - the housewives choice -and every election we have won since the war has been on the basis of a majority of the female vote"

All of this information has been clearly and succinctly laid before us, in research from both Lord Ashcroft (Smell the Coffee) and C-Change (The Case for Change). The prognosis is very clear – the patient may not be dead, but it is critically ill. Yet such an uncompromising picture of the position we find ourselves in should not simply be a prelude to much wailing and gnashing of teeth.

Three years ago, I famously told the Conservative Party Conference that many people saw us as 'the nasty party'. That comment won me a number of supporters, and also my fair share of critics. More importantly, the debate it was designed to trigger never happened. However, now three years later, following another crushing defeat, many in the party have realised that it is time for a great debate about the future of our party. The opportunity that Michael Howard has presented us with following his decision to stand down as leader has, for the first time, given everyone within the Party an opportunity to have a proper debate without fear or favour, without having to worry about provoking the wrath of the Party leader, or to what impact comments might have upon future job prospects.

Feminising the party

This may be the one and only opportunity we have properly to discuss and decide not only what kind of Party we want to be, but, more importantly, what kind of Britain we want to lead. It is so important that we as a whole Party make the right decisions, because the country needs a strong Conservative Party and a strong Conservative government more than it has for a quarter of a century.

So what choices do we have? What options are on the table? For many in the party that choice has come down to two options: modernisation or distinctiveness. But we do not have the luxury of an either/or. In fact not only are both modernisation and distinctiveness vital prerequisites of Conservative recovery, but we are in danger if we remain complacent about what they involve.

As I have said before, for so long as establishing 'clear blue water'- between us and them simply means 'completing the Thatcher revolution', 'marching on with privatisation', or 'finding the new Right to Buy' then the Conservative Party will remain out of touch with modern Britain. But equally, so long as 'modernising' remains nothing more than being 'less strident in tone', 'more caring' or 'nicer, younger, gayer, than the Tories of the 80s', then the Conservative Party will remain dead in the political water.

"Britain has changed. People's demands - and therefore the challenges political parties face have changed. It's time for the Conservative Party to catch up"

But even if we get all of this right, and we create a new, more modern, and more distinctive brand for the Conservative Party, we will still have a way to go. Specifically, we have to feminise both our party and our country.

Britain has changed. People's demands – and therefore the

challenges political parties face – have changed. It's time for the Conservative Party to catch up. Voters today may no longer be concerned about uncontrolled inflation, mass unemployment, and the threat of nuclear war. But these worries have been replaced by new concerns. People may be sick of hearing politicians spouting on about political philosophies and ideological approaches, but they do want to hear, in simple but optimistic and visionary terms, about how we will govern their country and what we will do to make their lives that little bit better.

We as politicians face a huge challenge. Over the years turnout has fallen, voter apathy is on the increase, and the trust that the public place in politicians is reaching dangerous levels. The task that MPs face in re-establishing the trust of the public is the same one that we as a party face if we are to reconnect with voters and win power again. This must begin by breaking down the comment that far too many of us hear on the doorstep: "politicians are only in it for themselves". If the vast majority think this to be the case, what then do they think about us as a party?

> "All politicians spend too much time talking about structures. In their everyday lives, people don't"

My view remains that we are not, and never have been, a nasty party. Looking around the candidates we fielded at the last election, talking to our councillors, or meeting our Conservative future members shows how wrong that stereotype is. Across the country, our party is full of bright, active, and very normal people! Yet the C-Change research I referred to earlier showed that 67% of people think we are out of touch and 58% think we don't care about ordinary people.

It is time to change the way that we as a Party are portrayed. But to do that, it is time that we changed the issues we focus on and the way we talk to the public. To move the Party forward we need (i) to abandon our traditional (and too often dismissive, negative, cynical, and ya-boo) approach to politics and adopt a new look, tone and approach, (ii) to adapt to the new politics and accept that that will involve communicating and campaigning in a whole new way, (iii) to be professional in the way we organise both our Parliamentary and professional parties, (iv) to be radical and inventive about how to make government and its structures work for people, and (v) to stop talking about narrow policy specifics and start talking about the kind of real-world outcomes that matter to everyday people. Above all else, and in everything that we say and do, we need to show people that we share their values and that Conservative ideas are about delivering a better life for all, not just for a few.

Making the lives of people better

All politicians spend too much time talking about structures. In their everyday lives, people don't. People talk about the quality of their lives, about how every day is a struggle, and about the real things – sometimes just the simple things – that a government could do to make their lives that bit easier. If we really want to find the silver bullet or identify the 21st century equivalent to 'Right to Buy', then we should be looking at how we as a party and, more importantly, as a potential government could do just that: make the lives of the British people easier and better.

> "A Ministry of the Family could cut across the barriers between different departments and show that we understand the needs of families caught in the trap of both dealing with childcare and caring for elderly relatives"

Of course, Tony Blair and new Labour talked a lot about joined-up government, but that is all they did. We too have often talked about cutting red tape and regulation, but we have failed to make the connection with the public about how or why we would be different.

People don't think like government, breaking things up in separate compartments. Got a question about childcare? go to this department. Got a question about work and benefits? go to that department. Got a question about health? ask another department. All too often, we ourselves (despite the fact that we are in opposition) still fall into the trap of talking like bureaucrats, interested only in process, rather than like people who understand what daily life is about. That's the reality of life for most people in Britain today.

To government and its bureaucrats, public services are a jumble of numbers, statistics, targets, structure, and systems. Not to the people who use them. They just know that if your childcare isn't available, you can't get to work; if you can't find a care home place for your elderly father, your life can be turned upside down; and if your GP surgery closes on a Saturday, the only thing you can do is go to a hospital or hope you're not worse by Monday.

Most people in this country think that government and 'officialdom' live on another planet. As far as they're concerned, government just doesn't get it. It makes everything so difficult, so complicated. If we could convince people that our approach in government would be radically different, then we may begin to convince people that we understand the issues that concern them, and that we are on their side.

Rather than talk about cutting back on government to save money (or – as voters would see it – to give more money to our rich cronies), we need a radical agenda to modernise government and make it work for people, not against them. We should begin to map out clearly how a Conservative government would operate to make their lives better. The breaking down of government silos might not sound sexy, but showing how government would work for people rather than against them is very enticing.

For example a Ministry for the Family could cut across the barriers between different departments and show that we understand the needs of families caught in the trap of both dealing with childcare and caring for elderly relatives. The aim is not bigger or smaller government for its own sake. The aim is government that works for people.

A long lasting commitment to public services

In 1979, the incoming Conservative Government was faced with the challenge of sorting out a poor economy that was failing a poor country. Today the challenge is to sort out a poor government that is failing a rich country. We need to re-focus government on what we as a nation want and what we need it to be doing now. That means not simply doing what Labour ministers or Whitehall bureaucrats think government should be doing. And it doesn't mean simply pledging to do what Conservative members thought was the right thing to do twenty years ago.

So structures matter. And intentions matter too. We Conservatives know that this country is stronger when people are stronger, when individuals and families have the freedom to make decisions for themselves, and when you decide your future, not the Government. We understand that a government should be there when you need it, but steps back when you don't. Yet the challenge is to make this case without people thinking it just means cuts to the NHS or to schools. Only when we once and for all make a long lasting commitment to the public services will we be able to convince people that our vision is their vision – that we share their values and that they can trust our intentions. That's why we should make our commitment to maintaining the best quality public services now. And we must go on repeating that belief every day for the next five years until people actually begin to believe it.

Reassembling the Jigsaw

Security is a word that has been used so often recently in relation to national security and law and order that other aspects are forgotten. Security doesn't just mean being safe as a country and safe in our own homes and streets, but also peace of mind. People want the peace of mind of knowing their child can get into the local school and that it will be a good school with a good level of education. They want the peace of mind of knowing their local hospital is a good one. They don't want their choice to drive the level of service in their school or hospital, instead they expect the level of service provided to be good in every school and hospital. If they want to exercise choice it is to choose between good schools or good hospitals, not to choose between the good and the bad. The Conservative Party has not yet woken up to this crucial point.

The pieces of the jigsaw

Ultimately, the Conservative Party needs an ambition, a vivid story of what life would be like in Britain under a Conservative government. We need to describe our vision: of a dynamic country where we all have the freedom to get on with our lives and make decisions for ourselves, our families and our communities; a can do society, where we all are encouraged and able to make the most of our opportunities; and a grown-up government, there when it's needed, and ensuring that none of us get left behind.

These beliefs should underpin all that we do. We must articulate them clearly. We must show how they fit today's world. Above all we must show that together they provide a clear and positive vision of hope for the future.

But unless people feel comfortable with us they will not trust us to deliver for them. That is why the changes to the look and approach of the Party must also be made and made quickly. Hence at the last election, although our policies were geared to provide freedom and opportunity through choice, voters felt that we simply were not the party for people like them. We told people we wanted to reward hard-working families who were doing the right thing, but they thought that meant doing what we thought was right, not what they thought was right. So a message we intended to be inclusive became exclusive.

Voters want to know that their politicians not only understand their lives, but are people like them. We must appear to be genuine, honest, authentic and decent people if voters are to be willing to listen to what we have to say and then to trust us to deliver on it. This is where how we dress, the language we use and the tone of our approach matter. If we look and sound like a group of people

Rt Hon Theresa May MP

divorced from the real world, then people just won't run the risk of allowing us to govern their country.

So there really is no silver bullet and no single policy idea that is going to sweep us into government. This is like a jigsaw. Unless we put all the pieces together – changing the way we look and the tone we adopt, listening to people, identifying the problems they face and finding Conservative solutions to them – then we will not win. Above all we must show we are the Party of the future not of the past. We must show how our core beliefs of freedom, opportunity and security fit today's world and provide all Britons with the promise of a better future.

If we restate our values confidently, and show that we understand how to apply them to Britain as it is; if we change our behaviour so we are less like what people expect politicians to be like ...then the people will start to say of us again: Yes, Conservatives are my kind of party.

Rt Hon Francis Maude MP
Chairman of the Conservative Party

Francis Maude was born in 1953 and has served as the Member of Parliament for Horsham since 1997. He served in William Hague's Shadow Cabinet as Shadow Secretary of State for Culture Media and Sport, Shadow Chancellor and Shadow Foreign Secretary. He was the MP for North Warwickshire from 1983 to 1992 during which time he was a minister at the Foreign & Commonwealth Office and Financial Secretary to the Treasury. Educated at Corpus Christi, Cambridge, he was a barrister and councillor on Westminster City Council prior to his entry into Parliament. He was appointed a Non-Executive Director of ASDA plc in July 1992; was a Director of Salomon Brothers from 1992 to 1993; a Managing Director of Morgan Stanley & Co Ltd from 1993 to 1997. He is married with five kids.

Values for a New Century

It is a truth now universally acknowledged that the Conservative Party is in want of change. No one who has ventured into the debate that Michael Howard so sensibly called for has argued that all we need is one more heave. Denying the need to change would amount to saying that we have been right all along, and the electorate itself needs to change.

The electorate of course already has changed. Our problem is that we as a Party have not kept pace with the country; we have lagged behind.

The case for change

Calls for change in the Conservative Party tend to trigger three responses. First, that it is a navel-gazing distraction from the real job of attacking our opponents. Second, that 'change' is code for aping Tony Blair. Third, that it means abandoning true Conservative principles in favour of a soggy and treacherous marsh called the middle ground.

> "The middle ground is treacherous terrain. It has always seemed wrong to me that a great party should seek to move either towards its opponents or away from them"

Let me deal with each in turn. No, of course we should not be endlessly picking the fluff out of our own navels. But we do have to get this analysis right. We do need to understand why not nearly enough people vote for us. At a time when people have lost faith in the willingness of politicians to be honest about anything, a clear willingness to be honest about our own problems really isn't a disadvantage.

Second, 'aping' Tony Blair. Labour's problems after 1979 were profoundly different from ours today. Their whole underlying ideology had been proved wrong both electorally and in substance. Our principles haven't. There is no Clause IV moment for the Conservatives, no single vivid emblem of change.

The third objection to change is that it is code for abandoning true Conservatism. I reject this. The middle ground is treacherous terrain. It has always seemed wrong to me that a great party should seek to move either towards its opponents or away from them. The doctrines of 'clear blue water' and 'the middle ground' are equally dangerous seductions. Both are wrong and for the same reason: that they require us to define our positions by reference to our opponents rather than by reference to our beliefs.

Values for a New Century

So our challenge is different from that faced by new Labour. It is to apply our beliefs to the problems that Britain faces today. It is to show that we understand modern Britain and the aspirations and concerns of modern Britons. There is plenty of evidence that people in Britain, especially younger people, are hungry for Conservative policies. Our problem is that they are depressingly reluctant to vote for today's Conservative Party.

> "So change is needed – to enable the Conservative Party again to fulfil its historic destiny, which is to place its values and beliefs at the service of our country and our communities"

We have lost support since 1997 among women, our electoral mainstay throughout the 20th century; among younger voters, where we are now in third place among voters under 35; among the A and B socio-economic groups; above a line from the Severn to the Wash; and in the great cities outside London.

When Margaret Thatcher won her first victory in 1979, Conservatives had a solid lead among women, younger voters and the fabled AB voters. She achieved this because she had herself modernised the Party. She had made our Party the most forward - looking; the Party most in tune with the way people, especially younger people, wanted to live their lives, and most in tune with the kind of Britain in which they wanted to live. She had understood that there is no conflict between 'traditionalists' and 'modernisers'; indeed that one of the greatest traditions of the Conservative Party is that it has always been instinctively ready to renew and modernise itself.

Today we are too often seen as a party at odds with contemporary Britain. Even among people who agree with us and vote for us, far too few answer yes to the question: "are the Conservatives my kind of party?" That's not because our principles and values are wrong. It's because they still think we're at odds with them.

So change is needed – to enable the Conservative Party again to fulfil its historic destiny, which is to place its values and beliefs at the service of our country and our communities.

Timeless conservative values

First we need to take our values and beliefs a lot more seriously. There is no single one imperative that dominates all others. I was not surprised that there was a mixed response when the Board of the Party recently proposed a set of values to be incorporated into the Party's constitution. Some found it hard to decide whether to criticise them for being hopelessly bland or for heralding some sinister repositioning. In truth they simply represented the best effort at distilling the timeless values to which any serious Conservative in the last fifty years or indeed the next fifty years would be happy to subscribe.

Strong communities

A lack of commitment to strong communities was perhaps the greatest aberration of the Conservative Government in the 1980s. Today almost everyone is a localist. But we should remember the localist heritage of our party. Lord Salisbury created the County Councils in 1888, while the 18th century Tories were the country party, believing in the dispersal of power. Since then we've had two major departures from Tory localist orthodoxy. The first was in response to the great centralising reforms of the Attlee government. Conservatives thought to reject the idea that the "gentleman in Whitehall knows best" was to risk caricature as the party turning its back on public services. The second aberration was Margaret Thatcher's determination to enforce good standards and financial discipline on left-wing councils.

> "The lesson for Westminster seems to be that when you lose your monopoly on power you gain a more satisfied electorate, with a far greater sense of involvement in and ownership of the political process"

In retrospect we can see that she was spot on in her analysis of the problem but wrong in her proposed solution. What should have happened then – and must certainly happen now – is a massive strengthening of local democracy.

This Government deserves praise for initiating mayoral elections in several parts of the country. The outcome has strengthened the hand of those of us who see a growing role for elected officials administering state resources and public services at a local level.

Many people are looking with renewed interest at the highly successful Swiss system of propositions and referenda. At local, state and national level it is citizens themselves who wear the trousers. They have the power to initiate action and to vote on matters of concern. The lesson for Westminster seems to be that when you lose your monopoly on power you gain a more satisfied electorate with a far greater sense of involvement in and ownership of the political process.

Let's pursue localism with rigour and enthusiasm. But we must understand that serious localism is no kind of soft option. If we are truly to let go from the centre, we have to accept that sometimes things will go wrong. Make hospitals genuinely independent and not all will perform to high standards. Letting go means you will get postcode policing, postcode prescribing, postcode recycling. Autonomy means real autonomy, not "earned autonomy", one of the more depressing phrases from the New Labour lexicon.

> "A society where so many people and communities are left behind, trapped in a hideous cycle of deprivation and failure, is a fractured and mean society"

Cohesive society

Second, we make a commitment to a cohesive society. Why do we need to spell it out? Because people came to think, because some Conservatives themselves came to believe it, that Conservatism was just about individualism.

It's easy to see how it happened. Turning Britain around in the 1980s required a decisive break with the state collectivism of the post-war era. But the alternative to state collectivism is not individualism. It is people doing things themselves, voluntarily. And that's what most of us do, day by day, in the family, at work, with friends, sports, church or voluntary organisations.

This is what makes such a thing as society. And Conservatives believe that the strength of society flows from what people do, not what the state does.

Personal Freedom and responsibility

This then flows into our third value: personal freedom and responsibility. The notion of personal responsibility - a phrase that trips with eager enthusiasm from Conservative lips - must include the responsibility that everyone has for each other and for society being genuinely cohesive. Iain Duncan Smith is completely right when he speaks of the need for Conservatives to talk the language of social justice, and to mean it. A society where so many people and communities are left behind, trapped in a hideous cycle of deprivation and failure, is a fractured and mean society, where we are failing in our personal responsibility for each other.

Limited Government

Fourth in the list is limited government. For me, part of this is a strong Conservative preference for lower taxes. The arguments are wearily familiar. Yes, you tend to get a stronger economy when taxes are lower. Yes, we do believe that people are likely to be more self-reliant, and look after themselves and their families when they pay less tax. But we also believe that society is likely to be stronger and more cohesive when taxes are lower. There is an economic case and a moral case for lower taxes. But at the best these arguments sound cold; at the worst they can sound like a self-interested appeal to the voter's own self-interest. By contrast the social case for lower tax is an idealistic appeal to people's best instincts. For the assumption it makes is that people generally want to do good and generous things. They have a sense of obligation to each other, to their communities and to people in need of help wherever in the world they may be.

It can be argued that this presumption is excessively optimistic. That there is less and less space in people's lives for altruistic activity, whether financial or physical. Maybe. But it's worth remembering that during the 1980s, when marginal tax rates fell sharply, charitable giving multiplied.

However, our commitment to the virtues of limited government must never be at risk of being parodied as a visceral hatred of the state and all its works. For one thing, Conservatives have always believed in a strong state able to do well those things that must be done by the state. That doesn't just mean the bare minimum: defence of the realm, maintaining the currency, securing public order and safety. It means a serious role in ensuring the provision of quality public services.

Conservatives will find it hard to take an appealing part in this hugely important debate if the perception persists that our only interest in the public services is in breaking them up, privatising them and helping people to escape from them. Even if the most radical dreams of the most creative Conservative reformer were miraculously to be implemented tomorrow, the truth is that most people's health-care and education in any kind of near term future is going to be paid for and provided by the state. It is well attested that people's generally warm approval of Conservative policies on health and education drops sharply when told that these are policies put forward by Conservatives. The problem is not our policies; the problem has been ourselves.

Our commitment to limited government has sometimes in the past inclined Conservatives to play down the importance of environmental policy. But "leave it to the market" won't quite do. Environmental degradation, as Oliver Letwin has recently argued, demoralises and degrades the human condition. While Conservatives will always and rightly prefer market-oriented solutions to environmental problems, let us never forget that even an emission-trading system requires a regulatory cap set by

Values for a New Century

government to be effective. It is the people who have made sure that politicians now have no alternative but to do what they can to make poverty history. The Conservative Party could today mobilise the same emotional commitment in the public to solving environmental problems.

When we talk about transport, it is no good us claiming that we are simply the party of the motorist. For one thing, it tends to confirm the negative perception that our values are essentially individualistic rather than social. On a more simplistic level it ignores the fact that most car drivers want better public transport. And we should accept also that even allowing for road pricing, which we should certainly support in principle, the stark reality is that the major improvements in transport infrastructure that Britain needs in order to be a cutting edge enterprise economy will not come about simply by the operation of the market and private finance. It will require activist government but also some serious commitment of taxpayers' money. So limited government, yes - but not minimalist government.

Established institutions

Number five is our commitment to established institutions. Of course that doesn't a blind reactionary attachment to any structures that happen to exist. But it does convey an understanding of the strength that society derives from institutions that have the authority and independence that flows from history. In relation to the constitution, it is the deep understanding of the complex and unwritten relationships, the checks and balances, that have evolved over centuries in an organic web of tradition, convention and practice.

> "We have to show that we understand that the family is a broader institution that the twentieth century nuclear model"

One such established institution is of course the family. No Conservative needs persuading that the family is essential social glue. Children are generally better with fathers as well as mothers. But we have to show that we understand that the family is a broader institution than the twentieth century nuclear model. The fact is that today many parents bring up families on their own. In the last few days of the election I had a salutary conversation with a highly articulate woman. She came from a Conservative family, and she wanted to vote for us, but couldn't bring herself to do it. 'Why?' I asked. 'Because I'm a single mother', she replied. There is a profound lesson for us. She was not out of sympathy with Conservative values but she was deeply out of sympathy with the Conservative

Party.

This is not particularly about whether or not we are social liberals. I happen to think we should not be a party that seems to lecture people on how they should live their lives. But my single mother in Crawley was not rejecting us because she thought we were illiberal. She was rejecting us because she thought we hadn't caught up with how people live their lives in modern Britain.

The rule of law

Sixth in the list is commitment to the rule of law. Conservatives believe in the rule of law not merely in the banal sense of obeying the law of the land but as a principle of a society in which law and the judicial process are not subjugated to the whims of politicians. As democrats, Conservatives will uphold the supremacy of the legislature over the judiciary, but this imposes a grave duty on those elected to Parliament not to collude with attempts to chop and change the law of the land for the political convenience of ministers.

This government has done two things that, taken together, now act as a pincer movement undermining respect for the law. Civil liberties as traditionally enjoyed in Britain have been undermined. We've seen trial by jury eroded, the law of double jeopardy compromised and ID cards proposed.

Britain is not to be a 'show me your papers' society. And we must not fall into the trap of making life difficult for everyone, including the innocent, because we are too timid to target and deal with the guilty.

The law is also being brought into disrepute by the implementation of the Human Rights Act. Judges have used its vague yet sweeping provisions to make a series of rulings that bear no relation to the intentions of legislators, the wishes of voters or common sense itself.

"Helping Africa is not a fashion statement, it's a moral imperative"

National Self-Confidence

Value number seven is national self-confidence. Conservatives believe Britain should look confidently outward - be internationalist, never isolationist. Apart from his love affair with the idea of European integration, a love affair now rudely interrupted, there is much to praise in the conduct of the Prime Minister. The Balkans, Sierra Leone and Iraq have all benefited from vigorous armed interventions either led by, or substantially contributed to, by the UK.

I referred earlier to the unstoppability of making poverty history.

Values for a New Century

Helping Africa is not a fashion statement, it's a moral imperative. How right Michael Howard was to put into our manifesto a commitment over time to increase Britain's international aid to the UN target of 0.7%. It gives us the moral authority to make the argument - the powerful argument - that aid and debt forgiveness alone are not the only solution to African poverty. Thirty years ago Asia had the same GDP per head as Africa. Today it's three times as high. Not because Asia has had more western financial aid than Africa. It hasn't. It is the direct result of liberalisation and democratisation. Africa must be helped along the same path. Here is the global challenge of the next decade. Corrupt and warmongering regimes must be helped aside and the dedication and generosity of the developed world allied to the natural talent and resources of Africans to improve the continent out of all recognition.

This kind of instinctive internationalism is the true basis of Conservative Euroscepticism. The noble vision of a united Europe developed by the post-war generation of politicians as a response to their own sombre experiences now looks a bit limited in ambition to the gap year young of the 21st century. The idea of an ever more centralised club on the western side of Europe with its outmoded head office culture is beginning to collapse under the weight of its own anachronisms.

Enterprise culture

Last comes a commitment to an enterprise culture. It ought to go without saying. But for too long we've tended to assume that once you do lower tax and deregulation you have a full Conservative economic policy. As both George Osborne and David Willetts have argued, our economic policy has to be far broader than that. Some product markets in Britain don't work well. A lot of things are much more expensive here than elsewhere. Supply side reform never comes to an end.

> "World class education is crucial to Britain being a really successful knowledge economy, and it won't just come about through the benign workings of the market"

Alongside our preference for limited government must be a recognition of the need for new thinking on education. World class education is crucial to Britain being a really successful knowledge economy, and it won't just come about through the benign workings of the market.

Rt Hon Francis Maude MP

Making us "My kind of Party"

So is it enough to have clear values, and to have thought out how they apply to modern day Britain? I don't think it is. I think the need for change goes further.

The political landscape has changed. People see conventional adversarial politics as being out of kilter with the reality. Most people - even if disillusioned with Blair and New Labour, as most are - do not feel especially threatened or alarmed by them.

So if we go on about the government as if it were the worst government ever, if we overstate and exaggerate the case against Labour, we trigger two responses from anyone still listening. One is that it confirms their view that we don't mean what we say which in turn makes it more difficult to secure a sympathetic hearing for anything at all we have to say.

The second typical response is that if we go on as if they think the country has actually ground to a halt then it simply confirms the perception that we inhabit a different universe.

I should stress that this is not a plea for soft-pedalling Labour. Where we think they're wrong - and they often are - we should say so. But when we think they're right or trying to get it right - and sometimes they are - we should say that as well. Being populist does not make you popular. Saying things that sound like they're being said in order to win votes is a turn-off.

It seems to be a rule of British politics that in order to achieve the scale of electoral sea change that defeating Labour requires always involves winning the support of younger voters. This was true in 1951 and 1979. The party that breaks a pattern has to be the party that is the more forward-looking of the two.

I have no doubt that Conservatives can achieve this again. Today younger people are more sceptical about government and the ability of government to improve their lives than my and preceding generations were. They simply do not believe that the state is going to provide for them. And at the same time they're much more self-confident about their own ability to make a difference. They want the state to concentrate on the things that only the state can do and give them more space to run their own lives.

But we have to cut through their scepticism about politics and politicians. We need the chance to persuade them that we mean what we say; that we will do what we say; and that we will do it not because it serves some narrow sectional interest, nor just because it creates a better and more vibrant economy, but because our way is the way to create a more generous, cohesive and compassionate society.

If we do all this: if we restate our values confidently, and show that we understand how to apply them to Britain as it is; if we change our behaviour so we are less like what people expect politicians to be like; if we are true to the best of ourselves; if we get out and stay out of our comfort zone, our geographic, social and cultural comfort zone; then people will start to say of us once again: "Yes, the Conservatives are my kind of party." Then we can begin - again - to serve our country in government."

The roots of the Conservative problem lie in the legacy of Thatcherism and a failure to recognise that the political landscape changed irreversibly in the mid - 90s…slowly and painfully the Party set out on a journey in 1997 which most refused to recognise was necessary, now we are around the half - way mark…we need to break with the past and accept that we need a change of attitudes and to bring in new people.

Archie Norman
Chairman, Energis Communications

Archie was the Member of Parliament for Tunbridge Wells from 1997 until 2005. He held various positions in the Conservative Party including Deputy Chairman, Chief Executive, Shadow Minister for Europe and Shadow Secretary of State for Environment Transport and the Regions. From 1991 to 2000 he led the successful turnaround of ASDA Group plc. Previously he was Group Finance Director of Kingfisher plc; Chairman of Chartwell Land; Partner at McKinsey & Co and at Citibank.

The Problem is Us

When in 1997 I decided to attempt to become the first ever FTSE 100 Chairman elected to the House of Commons many of my friends thought I had taken leave of my senses. But having tried my hand in the private sector, I wanted to put something back for my country and the Conservative Party. Naively, I believed the Conservatives could be back in power in five years' time. That was a pretty basic error. It was not until I became immersed in William Hague's early programme of reform that I realised how deeply rooted in its own culture and values the Conservative problem lay.

The Conservative delusion

Having left Parliament after eight years and reviewing the debris of my thwarted hopes from afar, two things strike me. One is how little the debate has changed. The arguments today, even the words, are not very different from eight years ago. They were debated in William Hague's Shadow Cabinet. Remember the much derided 'Kitchen Table' Conservatism amusingly written by Danny Finkelstein? Remember in 2001 Portillo's lofty and self-destructive campaign? Remember too the high ideals of Michael Howard's acceptance speech in 2004? The ideas have often been good ones but the old Party has always bitten back. What the general public see is 'same old Conservatives.'

"Conservatives talking about the future of Conservatives would seem rather more interesting if they started from an original analysis of the future of the country."

My second, not unconnected observation is how uninteresting Conservatives have become. Looking back at Westminster and the speeches which could have been of my making, I find it hard to motivate myself to listen. We are of course in a post-ideological era. But surely there must be something more original than to debate than old 'tug of war' arguments such as whether or not we should be committed to reduce taxation (kind of obvious). Despite eight years of Opposition the Right in Britain is still intellectually sterile. The great fission of debate, the infusion of new ideas from outside, the creativity and innovation that is needed to be interesting is still not there. Conservatives talking about the future of Conservatives would seem rather more interesting if they started from an original analysis of the future of the country.

The reason the Party has 'reverted to type' in three successive elections is because the attitudes and responses that emerge under

The Problem is Us

stress are deep in the culture. As a result many Conservatives even today remain in a state of denial about the extent of the problem. We have a cosy desire to believe that there is nothing fundamentally wrong: the problem is to do with everyone other than us. After 1997 Conservative orthodoxy had it that Tony Blair and New Labour were a fraud on the electorate, who had won by deceit and governed through spin.

> "Many Conservatives remain in a state of denial. We have a cosy desire to believe that there is nothing fundamentally wrong: the problem is to do with everyone other than us"

The latter version has it that they have failed to deliver and are in the process of wrecking the economy and eventually the public will rumble them. By implication our problem is not us. It is the electorate. Recently, leading figures have argued that there is nothing wrong with the personality or values of the Party. We just have to get the 'message' right.

These are different versions of the Conservative delusion. Our policies and the way we convey them reflect the values and attitudes that make up the Party today. A charismatic leader would be a small part of the solution. The conduct of leadership and the forces acting on the leader are forged by the people around him. A leader that understood the extent of the problem and is determined to change the mould is what is needed. You can't spray paint new enthusiasms and new policies on an old chassis. We have a fading brand driven by people who represent a diminishing minority of the general public some of whom radiate values which are not shared by much of contemporary Britain. The problem is fundamental and the problem is us.

Too many people still assume the Party is authoritarian, opportunistic, close-minded and out for itself. Not because they read the manifesto, but because that's how it 'feels' when Conservative spokesmen appear on television. In an era where politicians are not widely respected or listened to, only the most salient communication cuts through, so people understand we are anti-immigrant, anti-Europe

> "Conservatives are no longer exposed daily to the problems of urban Britain, of debt - ridden students, of failing schools, of our immigrant communities. Yet this is where Conservatism is most needed"

and anti a lot of things. They have seen no evidence that we are compassionate, interested in others, one nation, etc. Not only because there has been no evidence, but because in some cases we aren't.

Further, the Party base is still narrowing despite the welcome infusion of new blood at the election. It is critical to break out of the retreat from the North and urban centres. Yet the concentration of Conservative support into the affluent suburbs and rural areas of England continued at the last election. In the North East and North West our share of the vote fell. We now rank third amongst all people below the age of 35 and come third in more seats than ever in recent memory. The problem this narrowing of the base creates is that Conservatives are no longer exposed daily to the problems of urban Britain, of debt - ridden students, of failing schools, of our immigrant communities. Yet this is where Conservatism is most needed – in the parts of Britain where crime and state failure is depriving children of opportunity and vulnerable people of their liberty.

The first step in arresting the decline of any fading organisation is to fracture the old culture and give access to new ideas and new people. Britain is more Conservative than it has ever been. Any attitudinal test of 'young Britain' would reveal people to be more independent, more enterprising, more intolerant of authoritarianism or nanny state-ism than ever. Young people want to be able to get ahead in their lives, believe strongly in creating wealth to provide for others, etc... far from being Labour in their values, they are Conservative. It is we who have walked away. Our challenge is not to abandon Conservative principles it is to express them through the aspirations and attitudes of contemporary Britain.

Taking the party to the country

So my prescription for a revival is to bring an essentially Conservative public into the Party, and the Party to the country. We should start at the bottom. Conservatism should be rooted in community and in grass roots participation. It should be a popular Party as it was in the fifties and sixties not the exclusive dwindling band of loyalists it has become today. Most MPs think of the volunteer organisation as somewhere between a lost cause and a total liability. Yet almost all winning political movements have popular support in the form of an activist base, including George Bush's Republicans. And by activists I mean not just volunteer constituency members but the entrepreneurs, the academics, students, and pressure groups that make up Britain's political influence community. We need a new wave of popular reform to involve ordinary people. Removing them from the leadership franchise is not a good start. William Hague's aspiration to double the membership was the right one: we should cut membership fees to five pounds or less. We should drive, not abolish central membership and the email base, politicise our

The Problem is Us

8,000 councillors making them feel an enfranchised listened - to part of the Party. We should consider holding US - style primaries in selected constituencies for candidate selection. Outside the activist base we need to be far more vigorously open to participation. We should launch semi-independent Conservative satellite organisations on the University campuses and amongst special interest groups. In short, we should invite Conservative - thinking people of all walks of life to come and help us reforge the real Conservative Party.

Next we should address the Westminster disease. Of course as Conservatives we regard Parliament as the cradle of democracy and the mother of parliaments. But that does not mean it is the seat of popular politics. For most it is redolent of hierarchy, partisanship and outdated protocol. Yet for Conservatives more than any other Party Westminster holds a cultural grip on the Party. Huge efforts are made to ensure Conservative MPs stay in Parliament losing votes by huge margins and making unlistened to speeches recorded for posterity in Hansard. Interviews are given from College Green by self - important back benchers in suits with the image of Big Ben behind them. Westminster is a wonderful place. Its buildings, its status, and its procedure are intoxicating. But changing the Party requires getting out into the country and talking from Manchester, not Millbank.

> "We should consider holding US style primaries in selected constituencies for candidate selection"

> "We should encourage Conservatives to be innovative and individuals and be a little more generous in our attitude to dissent... sacking people for speaking their mind is not seen as an endearing trait for the modern Leader"

Parties and partisanship are intensely disliked by today's public. That's why the most popular politicians tend to be above party – or outside it. Ken Livingstone and Ann Widdecombe are respected because they are seen to be beholden to no one. We should encourage Conservatives to be innovative and individuals and be a little more generous in our attitude to dissent and indeed our attitude to each other. Sacking people for speaking their mind is not seen as an endearing trait for the modern leader. The time has come to give people permission to think and permission to speak out. The public want candour not partisanship – forthright decent politicians who want to do their best not just carry favour. The problem is not that Labour is popular, it is that the Conservatives are unpopular. The first question to ask before formulating any policy or appearing on television is not "how do we win votes?" but "what would we do if in Government?"

It is a sort of necessary ritual for Conservative leaders to assert there is nothing wrong with Conservative values and principles. I am not so sure. The values we associate as true blue today are not the values of the Conservative Party of Macmillan or Baldwin or Hume or Macleod. The neo-Thatcherite consensus that has dominated Conservative politics since 1992 has led to a view that the great problems of Britain have been resolved. And if they have not, all that is required is a heavy dose of the same. Yet large tracts of Britain do not enjoy the liberty and opportunities of people who live in leafy Conservative constituencies. Poverty and loss of opportunity is still a serious problem, but largely geographically defined. To give one simple illustration: over 50% of all crime, 71% of violent crime, 75% of failing schools, almost all substandard housing, most recent immigrants, a high proportion of teenage pregnancies are concentrated in about 40 major inner city areas of Britain. Yet what was the Conservative policy for inner cities at the last election? There is a vacuum in our thinking.

> "It is a sort of necessary ritual for Conservative leaders to assert there is nothing wrong with Conservative values and principles. I am not so sure"

Recently a leading Conservative MP said to me that he was struck at how far Labour people were associated with the leadership of social pressure groups such as the Autistic Society. He suggested we need to do the same to 'show we cared.' Wrong idea. Nothing could be worse and more obvious than a politician sidling up to good causes in the hope of giving the appearance of caring. Our challenge is to recognise that there are deep - seated social ills in Britain that badly need real attention, not to show we care but because they really matter to us and the future competitiveness of our country and the quality of life of our people.

Encumbered by our values

Perhaps the most vivid illustration of a values - based flaw in our attitudes lies in our antipathy to the public sector. It has become a post - Thatcherite axiom that public provision is to be derided as inefficient and a bureaucratic drain on the taxpayer. Of course Labour profligacy has added substance to the argument. Yet a competitive country must have competitive infrastructure and much of this will always be publicly provided. Public service should be a very Conservative ideal. Of course that does not mean we should not strive for better use of taxpayers' money and

The Problem is Us

introduce market disciplines where necessary. But public service ethos and motivation matters. Indeed the public service ethos used to be central to Conservative thinking. What could be more Conservative than to encourage people to devote their lives to educate the children of others or looking after the sick. It was we who created new models of public service when in office and liberated government agencies from central control. Most primary school teachers voted for Margaret Thatcher in 1979. Yet at the last few elections we have made public servants, roughly a quarter of the work force, our enemy. It may be prosaic but good government requires competent management. And competent management depends not just on structural solutions but also delegating authority, limiting political interference, and attracting and rewarding leadership and motivating people to work for the public good. Not characteristics easily associated with our recent past.

We should recognise too that in the 1980s and 1990s some part of the Conservative tax reduction was achieved only by under investing in health and education thereby passing the cost on to a future generation. We may not like it but Labour was right in saying we neglected investment in health and educational infrastructure. But the public enthusiastically accept that investing in public services and making them work well is a good idea.

> "We feel the old sense of community has been lost because of the erosion of traditional values, the family, and the 'English' cultural tradition. This 'dismal' view takes us very quickly to 'wind the clock back' prescriptions"

The third area where values - based obstacles hold the Party back is in social policy. The Conservative view of social policy tends to start with a 'dismal' view of modern society. We feel the old sense of community has been lost because of the erosion of traditional values, the family, and the 'English' cultural tradition. This 'dismal' view takes us very quickly to 'wind the clock back' prescriptions: because we, rightly, approve of family ideals we would like government to encourage them. This takes us one short step to tax incentives. And we are worried about the social destabilisation of communities and therefore want to limit immigration. The problem with both these attitudes is not that they are wrong but their salience in our thinking reflects a narrow, pessimistic diagnosis of the problem and a solution that speaks of a certain personality type. We all know people who bang on about immigrants and unmarried mothers and the woes of society. They are often outspoken, authoritarian and negative, and usually very boring. They are rarely fun to have around. By stereotyping ourselves we engender a negative portrayal of conservatism and a disapproving view of contemporary society. We appear keen to alienate people who came here from abroad or the third to a half of the children borne out of wedlock in an attempt to turn the clock back.

There is a role for a Conservative social values agenda but it should start with equal respect for all our citizens and a desire to improve on and rejoice in society as we find it today. Most young people think Britain is a pretty good place to be and certainly better than it was in our childhood. The 'dismal' agenda needs to be balanced with a forward - looking vision of how to compete in the world using our unique national skills, culture and assets. Every day quality of life issues, such as housing provision, pre-school education, teenage pregnancy, autism, early years education do have a bearing on competitiveness and our addressing them is not just a drain on the taxpayer.

> "There is a role for a Conservative social values agenda but it should start with equal respect for all our citizens and a desire to improve on and rejoice in society as we find it"

The 21st century does offer great opportunities for a conservative Britain. Why are we not the Party advocating more not less university education? Why are we not the Party seeking to deregulate the universities and prosecute a more vigorous science based agenda? Why are we not exploring ways of exploiting our world leadership in cultural media and artistic skills? Why are Conservatives not more closely associated any more with Britain's young entrepreneurs?

The roots of the Conservative problem lie in the legacy of Thatcherism and a failure to recognise that the political landscape changed irreversibly in the mid 90s. Slowly and painfully the Party set out on a journey in 1997 which most refused to recognise was necessary. Now we are around half way to the destination. Travelling the remainder means having the confidence to break with the past and accept that we need a change of attitudes, values and to bring in new people.

Reviving the Party requires too a degree of humility. Conservatism at its best has always been pragmatic and capable of adapting to change. Trenchantly held views of leading Conservatives from the Corn Laws to appeasement have proven to be questionable in the fullness of time. Conservatism is as much a way of looking at society and the relationship of individuals to the state as is a set of principles. At our best we are generous, believing in people, decent, and forthright and reflective of views that bind the whole nation. Britain wants Conservatism to be that again.

The Tory Party needs a simple, comprehensible identity that is both true to its own traditions and that will appeal to the public. If 'One Nation' did not exist we would be striving to invent it. Something so deep rooted in principle, and with a history of such obvious political success, is the real answer to so called New Labour.

Rt Hon Sir Malcolm Rifkind QC MP
Shadow Secretary of State for Work & Pensions

Sir Malcolm was born in Edinburgh in 1946. He was the Member of Parliament for Edinburgh Pentlands from 1974 – 1997. He re-entered the House of Commons as MP for the safe London seat of Kensington & Chelsea in 2005 and was immediately promoted to the front bench by Michael Howard.

Sir Malcolm has wide-ranging cabinet level experience, having served as Secretary of State for Scotland, 1986 - 1990; Secretary of State for Transport, 1990 – 1992; Secretary of State for Defence, 1992 – 1995; Foreign Secretary, 1995 – 1997).

Educated at Edinburgh University, he is married to Edith with a son and a daughter.

Back to the Future

There is a disturbing paradox in Britain today. It is one that must be addressed by all those concerned with the future of our country.

On the one hand, Britain is a vibrant, exciting country. Most of its people enjoy reasonable prosperity. There is greater opportunity than was enjoyed by previous generations. There is little internal strife and a great sense of tolerance and fair play.

> "There is a great unease both at home and abroad. Are we truly one nation at peace with ourselves and with our neighbours?"

Britain also seems comfortable in its relations with the wider world. London is a major international city. Visitors and migrants speak of Britain being more welcoming and relaxed than most other Western countries. Our language is the first language of the world. Our values, beliefs and culture are part of a universal whole.

However, there is another side to contemporary Britain. There is a great unease both at home and abroad. Are we truly one nation at peace with ourselves and with our neighbours? The reality is that, alongside our achievements - of prosperity, individual opportunity and open mindedness - we are grappling with serious and disturbing challenges both to our country and to the world of which we are part.

Domestic Concerns

At home we have seen the fragmentation of our society. The family unit has less relevance than at any time in our history. Many children are brought up by one parent; the elderly either look after themselves or are helped by the state; people are less aware of their neighbours. Charitable and voluntary organisations may be more active than ever before but so is the need for them and for their services.

We have become more sensitive, particularly in the last few weeks, to the unresolved problems and strains in the relations betweenthe ethnic communities for whom this country is home. We had assumed that the welcome absence of inter-racial violence had meant that the peaceful integration of immigrant and host communities was progressing well. The recent terrorist incidents have brought home to every ethnic community that there remains hatred and alienation that can produce unspeakable violence. It is too early to say whether such problems are restricted to a few individuals or whether they are symptomatic of a much wider cultural gulf within the nation as a whole which will need to be urgently addressed.

> "Against a background of considerable success in many fields we are fragmented and divided in others. We need a new dynamic to resolve our problems both at home and overseas"

Our national unity has also been challenged by the growth, over several decades, of Scottish and Welsh nationalism, by the unresolved issues of Northern Ireland and by the clear evidence of a renascent English identity. These trends can be seen as a healthy corrective to the excessive uniformity of the past century but they can also lead to a harmful fragmentation and unproductive rivalry in what is a small, highly populated island.

Overseas concerns

Internationally, we may be able to hold our head up high on many issues but we have not begun to resolve our relationship with our partners in the European Union. Likewise our unequal alliance with the United States gives us considerable influence but little real power and has its impact on how we are seen by the rest of the world. We consistently undervalue the potential of the Commonwealth and we are distant from the growing power of China. The world has become a much smaller place and we will need to adapt accordingly.

So the country has formidable challenges. Against a background of considerable success in many fields we are fragmented and divided in others. We need a new dynamic to resolve our problems both at home and overseas. That dynamic for Britain can best be expressed as One Nation in One World.

What is the answer?

This is, of course, a belief and an aspiration and not a policy but its adoption would enable us to frame a strategy for both domestic and global challenges not in a vacuum but with an ideal and a principle to guide us.

It is no coincidence that this challenge for the nation and that faced by the Conservative Party have much in common. The Tories have, after all, been an integral part of Britain's history for centuries. In recent times Conservatives have had great success. They have won the battle of ideas. It has been Tory values of personal responsibility and Conservative belief in free enterprise and low taxation, that have become the common currency of all the political parties. Socialism and other ideologies of the Left have been irreversibly rejected.

But as with the nation as a whole, Conservatives have to recognise that past glory is no substitute for current performance. And just as the country as a whole needs to clarify its national identity and to build on its natural strengths, so the Conservative Party must respond in a comparable fashion to the challenges it faces. The remedy may not be all that different for the Conservatives as for the country. Let me explain why I believe this.

We are this year celebrating the 60th anniversary of the end of the Second World War. The main architect of victory in that conflict was Winston Churchill. Despite his achievement the Conservative Party was overwhelmingly rejected by the electorate in the General Election immediately afterwards. The reason was very simple.

For the public, the Tories were identified with the Depression of the 1930s, unemployment and with the means test. They did not seem right for the post war challenges of 1945. Churchill had won the War but he had lost the political battle. It seemed likely that the Conservatives would be out of power for many years.

"Churchill did not wait for 'one more heave'; he did not simply restate existing manifesto commitments. Instead, he set out to win the battle of ideas"

The parallel with the challenge facing the Conservative Party today is striking. Conservative ideas on free enterprise, personal responsibility, the role of the private sector and low tax have become so accepted that Tony Blair has been happy to wrap himself around them in order to win three elections. We have won the war but we have lost the battle since 1997.

Churchill did not wait for 'one more heave'; he did not simply restate existing manifesto commitments. Instead, he set out to win the battle of ideas. He established what became known as the 'One Nation Group' under Rab Butler, Enoch Powell, Iain Macleod and Reggie Maudling. They were so successful in creating a modern, relevant Conservative Party that six years later Labour was out and the Tories were in for 13 years.

"A clear commitment to One Nation Toryism would demonstrate that the Party feels an ethical and political obligation to the nation as a whole and not merely to our own supporters or to those who share our beliefs"

We must learn from our own history. As Tom Paine once said: "We now have it in our power to make the world again." We should do so by wearing One Nation as a badge of pride but we need to modernize and adapt it to the new world in which we live both at home and abroad.

Our enduring principle

The One Nation tradition of the Tory Party has its origins in Disraeli's concern about the Two Nations of the rich and the poor. While the elimination of residual poverty remains a priority for the Conservative Party as for the country, One Nation, today, has a much wider resonance and relevance.

At present, Conservatives are widely seen as speaking to ourselves and not to the wider country. We are, unfairly, caricatured as representing the interests of the 'haves' without any real commitment to the 'have - nots'. We are presented as the party of the South-East but without real roots in the Midlands, the North of England, Scotland or Wales. Historically, these canards are groundless but, today, they are widely believed and they have to be disproved.

Our commitment to controlled immigration and a firm policy on bogus asylum seekers may be right and in the national interest but we are widely seen amongst the ethnic minorities as largely indifferent to their aspirations. The result is that our share of the ethnic minority vote remains derisory.

- A clear commitment to One Nation Toryism would demonstrate that the Party feels an ethical and political obligation to the nation as a whole and not merely to our own supporters or to those who share our beliefs.

- It would give much-needed credibility to our policy on the elimination of absolute poverty and deprivation, and show that it reflects our values and not just tactical convenience.

- It would help persuade black and Asian Britons that the Conservative Party can be their party and that their involvement will be welcomed at every level of the Party.

- It would enable us to reach beyond the South-East of England and rebuild support in the Midlands, the North of England, Scotland and Wales. We are a national party or we are nothing. At present we are not a national party.

- It would recover our reputation as a party that prizes common sense and pragmatism over ideological fervour and show that we draw our support from timeless values, principles and beliefs and not from temporary political fashions.

- It would appeal to younger voters and show that we are a Party with idealism and vision, free from dogma, and with principles and a programme that can transform their future.

- It would enable us to develop a foreign and international policy that applies One Nation principles to the challenges of One World, and frees the Conservative Party of any Little Englander image. Recent weeks have reminded us all that millions of Britons identify with the plight of Africa and other poor nations. As Tories we share that concern and accept a moral and ethical obligation to improve the lot of our fellow man. In a previous age Conservatives led the national debate in seeking to improve 'the condition of the people'. Today, for the people, read the developing world but the obligation remains the same. The principles of One Nation are the same as those who seek the stability and contentment that would be achieved by One World.

- One Nation would, therefore, provide again, but in a modern and contemporary form, both real and symbolic evidence to the electorate that the Tory Party has changed and that those who consider themselves to be uncommitted to any political party can, with confidence and without troubled conscience, turn to us and give us their political support.

- It would also create the trust that is essential between the electorate and the Party if we are going to be able to introduce the radical policies on health, education, tax reform and reduction in the power of Whitehall, that are essential if the country is to move forward.

Consequences for the Party

"If 'One Nation' did not exist we would be striving to invent it"

We are in the middle of a great debate about the future of the Party. Some of our opponents will attempt to mock that debate and to ridicule those who are taking part in it. If we are wise we can demonstrate that we are behaving as mature, sensible adults determined to give the public a real and attractive choice so that Labour can be removed at the next election.

If the Tories are seen, at the conclusion of this debate, to have rejected a narrow - minded, self-centred, insular politics in favour of a return to an inclusive, moderate One Nation Toryism we will have sent a clear and unmistakeable message to millions of our fellow citizens that we have heard what they have been trying to tell us for the last eight years.

The Tory Party needs a simple, comprehensible identity that is both true to its own traditions and that will appeal to the public. If One Nation did not exist we would be striving to invent it. Something so deep rooted in principle, and with a history of such obvious political success, is the real answer to so-called New Labour.

But One Nation in One World is also a creed and an aspiration for the country as a whole. It recognises the need for diversity to thrive within a united country, for localism to revive within a United Kingdom, and for internationalism to flourish within a united world.

One Nation in One World

One Nation in One World is what the modern Conservative Party stands for. It is also an ideal with which the United Kingdom, as a whole, can identify as we address, together, the unprecedented challenges of our time.

"The Conservative Party, it is said, cannot win another election unless its values more closely match the values of the electorate. That may well be true... the Conservative Party's problem right now seems to be that it just doesn't know what it's for. No pollster can help with that."

Stephan Shakespeare
Joint CEO and Founder, YouGov plc

Stephan Shakespeare is Joint CEO and founder of YouGov plc, which since May 2000 has grown to become internationally recognised as the pioneering internet - based research company. Prior to YouGov, he was a teacher - principal for a school in Los Angeles, and Head of Special Needs in a Lambeth comprehensive. He has written extensively on education policy for the national press.

Stephan was educated at St Peters College, Oxford and is married with two daughters. He was the Conservative candidate for Colchester in the 1997 general election.

No Easy Way Out

Beware the pollster with a political agenda. The pollster appears to speak with the authority of a thousand people, indeed a whole nation. But as it is perfectly possible – deliberately or, more likely, inadvertently – to frame questions in a way that leads to an outcome closer to one's desires, the strongest caution must be urged if it becomes clear that a pollster does indeed want a particular outcome, or has strong views about a particular way forward.

Lord Ashcroft argued, in 'Wake Up And Smell the Coffee', that the Conservative Party must start paying due regard to evidence – polling evidence – and not simply rely on its prejudices and fantasies. He is of course quite right. But that places huge stress on the question: what is 'evidence'? Obviously reliance on spurious, prejudice-driven polling is worse than reliance on simple prejudice, since the first is the same as the second, except with fake authority. So what should be the criteria for polling evidence?

"Reliance on spurious, prejudice - driven polling is worse than reliance on simple prejudice"

We all know that the wording of questions can make a big difference to the response. In experiments conducted in the eighties in America, 20 to 25% of respondents said that too little was being spent on "welfare", while 63 to 65% thought too little was being spent on "assistance to the poor".

Equally important to the quality of 'evidence' offered by a poll is the context, including the range and preponderance of the questions asked. Survey design which reflects the interests of the pollster will be more likely to elicit the responses he or she is expecting. Adjacent questions can have a big effect. Again, in an experiment conducted in America (in 1950), half of a randomly split sample was asked "Do you think the United States should let communist newspaper reporters from other countries come in here and send back to their papers the news as they see it?" 36% said "yes". The second half of the sample were asked "Do you think a Communist country like Russia should let American newspaper reporters come in and send back to America the news as they see it?" 90% said "yes". They were THEN asked the same question as before – and the number who thought the communist newspaper reporters should be allowed to report from America went up from 36% to 73%!

What is the "true opinion" of the population in these cases? The first question was perfectly 'legitimate'. The second pair of questions was also 'legitimate'. Which results truly reflected public opinion? These questions must be uppermost in one's mind when reading anything offered as 'polling evidence'.

One pollster may regard sexual relations as the pre-eminent issue of our times and his/her polls will foreground concerns on this as if they were a key driver of political opinion. Others, like myself, might think perceptions of class, poverty and wealth are much more important, and polls designed by me might give these issues undue prominence. Research that I have designed strongly suggests that the Conservative Party's fundamental problem is that it is perceived by crucial swing voters as existing to defend the interests of the rich, while Labour and the Liberal Democrats are perceived as being more on the side of ordinary people. While I certainly agree that the Conservative Party should 'look and feel' more like the whole population and not just a small segment of it, I regard the current 'modernising' agenda as flawed because, by focusing on secondary-level issues as if they were primary drivers, it undermines the case for more fundamental re-appraisal.

> "Others, like myself, might think perceptions of class, poverty and wealth are much more important, and polls designed by me might give these issues undue prominence"

But I may very well be wrong - and that is my point about polling: what can we regard as 'evidence' when the survey-design is down to people who are themselves politically engaged? In my view, the best way to guard against the potentially dangerous error of pollster/client-agendas is to give the main authority to three kinds of research:

> "what can we regard as 'evidence' when the survey-design is down to people who are themselves politically engaged?"

Making polling work

- time-series research - that is, where the same question or series of questions is asked regularly of a comparable sample in a comparable setting over a long period of time. In absolute terms, the data may be wrong - but patterns of change up or down, or indeed a lack of change, will tend to be meaningful.
- comparing responses from differently-designed questions and contexts, using random split-sampling. Asking one half of the sample one question, and the other half the same question but with a single word changed. Or exactly the same question but in a different context. Again, in absolute terms, the data may not be reliable, but the difference between the split samples can provide

genuine insight.

- deliberative research, where the design of the survey is rich enough to allow the respondent to consider several different aspects of the question and to some degree explore the issue, and relate it to a defined context. We rarely base our decisions on 'top-of-the-head' reactions to a quick question when randomly disturbed by a stranger on the telephone.

I apply this, of course, only to issues of highly complex motivation, such as political choices. Unless polling attempts to come closer to the disciplines of science - not just in fieldwork methodology but also in survey design - it is hazardous to claim for it the status of 'evidence', however interesting its results may sometimes seem.

Once we are satisfied that our research can produce proper, actionable evidence, then politicians still have to ask themselves, What do we need evidence for? Is it to make communication of our mission more effective, so that we are more likely to win the arguments we care about, or is it actually to define our mission in the first place? Recent debates on the future of the Conservative Party have implied the latter. The Conservative Party, it is said, cannot win another election unless its values more closely match the values of the electorate. That may well be true. But to alter your values to what opinion polls suggest is needed to win says something profound about your reason for being in politics. It suggests that your purpose in seeking political office is to get yourself a job you covet, rather than to advance a cause in which you truly believe.

"To alter your values to what opinion polls suggest is needed to win says something profound about your reason for being in politics"

The Conservative Party's problem right now seems to be that it just doesn't know what it's for. No pollster can help with that.

We should challenge Labour for the centre ground of British politics. We should combine the dynamism of personal freedom in a flexible economy, with recognising our obligations to others in a cohesive society. This is the authentic Conservative tradition.

David Willetts MP
Shadow Secretary of State for Trade & Industry

David Willetts has been the Member of Parliament for Havant since 1992. He served as Paymaster General in John Major's Government and has been a Shadow Secretary of State since 1998.

Oxford-educated, he has worked at HM Treasury, the Number 10 Policy Unit and the Centre for Policy Studies. He is a Visiting Fellow of Nuffield College, Oxford, a member of the Council of the Institute for Fiscal Studies and a member of the Global Aging Commission.

He is a keen walker and swimmer and is married to Sarah Butterfield, the artist and has two children.

A 20/20 Vision For Britain

Speeches on Conservatism are rather like London buses: you don't see one for ages and then they all come along together. But it is a good thing that the Conservative Party is at last debating its future, after eight years when we worried that such a debate would make us appear divided or disloyal.

> "We should challenge Labour for the centre ground of British politics. We should combine the dynamism of personal freedom in a flexible economy, with recognising our obligations to others in a cohesive society."

But there are some dangers in the way the debate is going. For a start it is in danger of becoming too bland. There really are some quite difficult questions here about our future strategy which can't just be resolved by us all pledging to be compassionate and forward looking.

Unless we do this people may be left in much the same perplexed state as the Duke of Wellington nearly 200 years ago, who said:

'We hear a great deal of Whig principles and Tory principles and Liberal principles and Mr. Canning's principles; but I confess that I have never seen a definitive account of any of them, and cannot make myself a clear idea of what any of them mean.'

We need a clear framework so that people know exactly what we stand for and how we can make Britain a better place. I believe there is a vivid way of setting out these challenges. We should challenge Labour for the centre ground of British politics. We should combine the dynamism of personal freedom in a flexible economy, with recognising our obligations to others in a cohesive society. This is the authentic Conservative tradition. We could do better than Labour, both when it came to a stronger economy and a better society. Above all, this should not be an inward looking exercise: we should look outwards, offering a positive vision of Britain.

A dynamic and flexible economy

The next election could well be called in 2010 - after all, Labour won't dare call it in 2009 if they are behind in the polls. And at the next election we should be offering a picture of what we can achieve for our country over the coming decade - our 2020 vision for Britain.

Our opponent is very likely to be Gordon Brown. He is the one who has dominated the political debate for a decade. It is he we must hold to account for the failures of his policies - from tax credits to pensions. It is a better alternative to Brown's Britain that we must articulate. We can already see how our vision can rival his. It is true that Britain now enjoys some macroeconomic stability. But what has Gordon Brown achieved with it? There has been nothing to compare with the big supply side reforms of the 1980s, reforming Trade Unions and privatising the nationalised industries. In fact it is increasingly clear that he has shirked all the big decisions.

The pensions crisis has not been tackled - all we get is endless consultation documents. And there is a growing energy crisis that could be manifested in peculiarly well named Brown-outs. As every day passes, it becomes clearer that he has lost control over the public finances and that is why this week he has had to fiddle the length of the economic cycle to try to meet the fiscal rules he himself invented.

"Gordon Brown has had to fiddle the length of the economic cycle to try to meet the fiscal rules he himself invented"

Everyone says of Tony Blair that with a large majority and a stable economy he had enormous opportunities to achieve big things but instead he has let that historic chance slip through his fingers. But the same is surely true of Gordon Brown. Where are the big decisions to spread personal ownership and opportunity? If anything Britain is becoming a less mobile society. Gordon Brown may try to help the poorest people, but there is another group, just above them, who are trapped in a intricate web of Tax Credits and high marginal rates for the withdrawal of benefits. It is worthy of Kafka, who did after all begin as an official working on industrial disability benefits.

We need a new generation of investment in energy, transport, and water, but we haven't got the right neutral regulatory regime for that. Instead the Government interferes to back favoured industries like wind farms and undermine others, like Railtrack. And where is the surge in business investment that we need to raise our productivity? New OECD figures show that the amount we produce per hour we work is way below many of our competitors. So there is much for Conservatives to offer on economic policy, going beyond tax cuts, however desirable. We need an economy that is more robust, open, and progressive than it is under

"This shifting of burdens from one generation to the next is a threat which links our critique of this Government's economic policy with our belief in a cohesive society"

Gordon Brown.

Instead of tackling the big problems today, Gordon Brown is shifting all the difficult decisions, not to mention the debt to finance his spending on to the next generation. In fact I sometimes fear that as class war disappears from British politics then generational war could replace it. This shifting of burdens from one generation to the next is a thread which links our critique of this Government's economic policy with our belief in a cohesive society.

A cohesive society

One of the great strengths of the Conservative tradition is that we understand the ties and obligations that link us across the generations. Economic policy should deliver equity between today's and future generations. Or, to put it rather more poetically as Burke did, the state ought to be "a partnership not only between those who are living but between those who are alive, those who are dead, and those who are yet to be born."

This same principle applies to social policy as well. Surely one of our deepest desires is that we should pass on values and principles from one generation to the next. The dominant way of thinking about British society now is to assume that we are fragmenting into atomised individuals with much weaker connections to others - and what better way to show we understand the weakening of these ties than by going tieless? Nobody appears to dispute this model, it is just that Conservatives can't appear to agree whether this is a good thing or a bad thing.

Fortunately, the truth is that we still have a powerful sense of obligation across the generations. The majority of adults with a surviving parent see them at least once a week. Grandparents are providing money to their families that is worth almost as much as Child Benefit. Most of us still aspire to get married and have children, even if sometimes we change the order round. Beneath the surface of a drunken, libidinous teenager clubbing on a Friday night, you will find someone who wants a decent job, a home of their own, and a strong marriage. Even if we start our adult life as if it is episodes from "Friends," most of us end up more like "The Simpsons."

Let me give an example of what this means in practice. We shouldn't just think of the problems of our deprived areas in terms of social mix but age mix. They have amazingly high numbers of children relative to adults. Across the country as a whole there are four adults to every child. In some of our problem estates children outnumber adults. And there are very few older people. William Golding's *Lord of the Flies* is a picture of what happens when children can run amok. A series of random decisions on housing and social security policy has created a state where a mix of generations has been lost. Restoring that by very different policies for the allocation of social housing would restore social cohesion as well.

My personal definition of a Conservative is a free marketeer with children. If we can capture the commitment to economic dynamism and social cohesion we will once more have a compelling message for the country. That is why I believe it is worth fighting for the future of our Country and my Party.

By the time today's primary school children leave university the balance of economic power in the world will have shifted dramatically. Economically Europe could even become a backwater, a bit part player on the world stage. Avoiding this painful and humiliating fate requires urgent action.

Tim Yeo MP

Tim Yeo has been the Member of Parliament for Suffolk South since 1983.

Tim served as a member of the Shadow Cabinet from 1998 to May 2005, and shadowed Health, Education, Trade & Industry, Culture Media & Sport and Agriculture and Environment and Transport.

Before entering parliament Tim was Chief Executive of Scope from 1980 to 1983, having previously held a number of posts in business. He founded the Charities Tax Reform Group in 1983, acting as Chairman until 1990. He was educated at Charterhouse and Emmanuel College, Cambridge.

Decline and Fall

Sadly but realistically the next Conservative Government won't take office before 2009 at the earliest. The problems it will address will be those of the second decade of the 21st century. More important, therefore, in terms of preparing for power, than all the internal agonising which is now taking place within the Party about whether we should immediately sound more robust about tax cuts or about how health care can be provided more efficiently, are the huge economic, environmental and political challenges which will dominate the political agenda in that decade.

Facing the challenge from the Far East

The economic challenge is one which business is starting to grapple with, but whose urgency the Labour Government has shown no sign of recognising. It is the rapidly intensifying global competition which is affecting services and manufacturing industry alike. This is a challenge for the whole of Western Europe, not just for Britain, and over the next few years it threatens the biggest and fastest ever transfer of investment and jobs away from Europe to the East.

"Economically Europe could even become a backwater, a bit part player on the world stage"

The population of China and India together is more than six times that of Europe. By the time today's primary school children leave university the balance of economic power in the world will have shifted dramatically. Economically Europe could even become a backwater, a bit part player on the world stage. Avoiding this painful and humiliating fate and ensuring our survival as a prosperous nation, remaining in the premiership economically if you like, requires urgent action on three fronts.

The first need is for a tax and regulatory system that is sympathetic to business and job creation. Tony Blair understands the rhetoric but has failed on the substance of this and the situation is made worse because so much of what the European Commission does is actively unhelpful. Without low taxes and lighter regulation, Britain will be starved of new investment in a world where capital is more mobile than ever. Business investment is already falling, although Gordon Brown characteristically fiddles the figures, and the sooner this is recognised and policy altered, the better our chances of preserving prosperity for our children.

The second task is to modernise our infrastructure. Our transport

Decline and Fall

system has for years been denied the investment it needs by governments of both colour. It has now become depressingly third world in terms of both quality and performance. Congested roads, unreliable trains and overcrowded airports don't just add to business costs, they are a deterrent to doing business here at all. Industries like financial services, where Britain is still world class, will continue to be important in this century but will only stay in London if the infrastructure is kept up to date.

> "The eastward shift of economic power will, within a generation, mean that Europe is economically dwarfed by the Asia Pacific region"

The investment needed for this modernisation will be private. Road users will increasingly have to pay charges, something they are willing to do in return for real improvements. Finding the capital to bring the railways into the 21st century without burdening taxpayers or passengers is possible as long as we insist that brownfield land around stations and railway lines is developed before greenfield sites. Developers won't welcome this but the environmental benefits will be huge. However, transport projects take a long time to reach fruition and we need to start on this today, not tomorrow.

Thirdly we must raise our game educationally. To be competitive in future Britain will need a far better skilled workforce, able to do the high value added jobs by which a mature successful economy will be characterised in future. More private and public investment in recruiting and retaining top quality teachers, substantial improvements in higher education (which would be enhanced by giving universities more freedom) and a stronger research and science base are all desperately needed. Robust examination standards in schools would help, too, instead of the absurdity of ever rising numbers of A grades at A level.

> "Education itself could become a significant visible and invisible export earner, and create goodwill towards Britain among influential citizens of other nations"

Education itself could become a significant visible and invisible export earner, and create much goodwill towards Britain among influential citizens of other nations because students almost invariably harbour warm feelings about countries other than their own where they have studied. Attitudes to industries from which we could earn our living in future need to change too. The world's consumers will spend more on sport and media than in the past, for example, two areas where Britain has natural advantages.

Tim Yeo MP

Saving the planet

The environmental challenge is climate change, a good issue for Conservatives to lead on because it's about responsible stewardship of the world's natural resources and the solutions involve using the market to influence behaviour while also offering business opportunities. Before we can grasp those, however, we need to accept the urgency of the problem. Doing nothing until the most hardened sceptics accept that human activity is one cause of climate change runs the risk that if timely action is not taken now, the cost of tackling the problem will rise substantially and the necessary lifestyle adjustments may be painful.

Climate change is going to be continuously on the political agenda for the foreseeable future and is another area where Tony Blair is good at the rhetoric but bad on the substance. One immediate task is to establish a more constructive dialogue with America. President Bush is right to insist that technology can provide answers to climate change but wrong to reject the use of targets for carbon emission reductions because they're a powerful spur to accelerate the very technology he wants and we should support the politicians and businesses in America who want to change the Administration's mind.

Britain could lead the world on all this but before we can once more exercise the influence we enjoyed under Margaret Thatcher we must put our own house in order. Under the last Conservative Government carbon emissions fell in Britain while the economy grew. Under Labour economic growth has continued but carbon emissions are now rising and the targets the Government itself has set may not be reached. What's needed is the courage to reshape our transport and energy policies.

In transport the attractions of low emission vehicles could be boosted dramatically by more generous tax incentives. Revenue generated by higher Vehicle Excise Duty (VED) and road user surcharges on high emission cars could be used to cut VAT, VED and user charges on greener models. Aviation, the fastest growing source of emissions in the transport sector, needs similar radicalism. Tony Blair failed to seek international agreement on an aviation fuel tax at the G8 summit, but action could begin with higher Air Passenger Duty, related directly to emissions, on domestic flights.

Once Britain starts acting to cut its own emissions it can better influence the debate on what happens next. This may involve more robust and widespread emissions trading and eventually a

Decline and Fall

move towards the contract and converge principle, one way to share the cost of achieving climate stability, a precondition for long term economic growth, fairly between rich and poor nations. At the same time British leadership on climate change would increase the chances that our own entrepreneurs could seize the business opportunities that will follow wider understanding of the challenge.

As soon as climate change is seen as a business opportunity, not a threat, progress towards the solution will accelerate. Cars and homes should be producing zero emissions within our lifetimes. Greater investment in energy efficiency, encouragement for energy crops as an alternative to food production for our farmers and a more vigorous and imaginative approach to the development of renewable energy all offer potentially profitable opportunities. Labour's inaction on all three, however, has made the need for another generation of nuclear power stations unavoidable.

Balance of power

The political challenge is the hardest of the three challenges to tackle. Understanding it requires a greater sense of history than Tony Blair has displayed in the last eight years which is probably why it's been assiduously ignored. We are on the threshold of a turning point in international relations. The collapse of the Soviet Union has meant that for the time being supreme political power is exercised by the United States alone. The last five years have made painfully clear that an American President does not need to listen to anyone, not even to their most loyal and supportive allies.

At the same time the eastward shift of economic power will, within a generation, mean that Europe is economically dwarfed by the Asia Pacific region. Political power will then gradually shift eastwards as well. America's engagement with Europe may turn out to have been confined to the century following its entry into the first world war, an anomaly in the great sweep of history. There is every reason to assume that America will increasingly look westwards towards China and Asia generally, as California has been doing for some time.

This leaves Europe extremely vulnerable. It's not fanciful to suppose that by mid-century the G8 summits will be considering Europe as a supplicant for aid, not a donor. Good economic management could avert that threat and maintain living standards but the political challenge will still exist. Europe, Africa and the Middle East will be weak in a world dominated by the super regions of the Americas and the East. Anyone who thinks that the so called special relationship will protect Britain in this situation hasn't travelled enough in the United States recently.

Unfashionably I believe the answer to this challenge is more cooperation between Britain, Germany and France. These countries have over two hundred million people who could remain among the richest in Europe. Acting together they might just retain enough clout to force America and China to pay attention. Acting separately they will not. At present serious shortcomings in the European Union, including its fanciful but mistaken foreign policy aspirations, are an obstacle to cooperation between the three most important countries but this shouldn't stop us considering how it could be achieved.

If the Conservative Party spent the next year or two examining these challenges and suggesting how they should be tackled it would look to disinterested observers as though it was serious about returning to government. Of course detailed policies on many other subjects would be needed but I am not optimistic about winning an election in 2009 just on the basis that we would run the public services better than Labour, even though I'm sure we can, or on a simple tax cutting agenda, however much that will be needed then.

The three challenges I've outlined are profoundly important to the future of every citizen. They determine whether he or she has a decent standard of living, lives on a planet that takes proper care of itself and in a country which still has influence in the world. They are challenges to which Tony Blair is not at present responding and to which the solutions are inherently Conservative ones. The electoral impact of being seen to take them seriously are therefore good.

"For the next four years let us seek bipartisan solutions and look for where we can support Ministers in the national interest, before we criticise or attack"

One final plea concerns the manner in which we conduct opposition. If there is one message above all other which is now coming very strongly from voters it is that people are fed up to the back teeth with partisan political point scoring. The politicians who will win in the future are those who are not afraid to agree with their opponents, who support the government when it does the right thing, even if that is unpopular. For the next four years let us seek bipartisan solutions and look for where we can support Ministers in the national interest, before we criticise or attack.

Decline and Fall

This requires a completely new mindset. It involves abandoning most of the assumptions on which Central Office has been operating for generations. But it would do more than anything else to convince the millions who have written off our Party in the last ten years that we are beginning to understand the world of the 21st century, willing to accept changes in how politics should be conducted and ready to rejoin the human race. Ready, in fact, to resume the government of our nation.

About the Bow Group

Since its foundation the Bow Group has had three aims: to promote ideas and debate on the centre right; to provide a forum for its members to meet and discuss policy; and to provide a platform for its member to communicate with senior figures in the Conservative Party. The Bow Group has no corporate view. The views expressed in Bow Group publications are those of the authors and do not represent the views of the Group as a whole or the Conservative Party. For more information about the Bow Group, please visit www.bowgroup.org

Membership

Membership of the Bow Group costs £40, with a concessionary rate of £20 for those in full time education, unemployed or under 25.

For more information,
visit www.bowgroup.org
or call 020 7431 6400

Sam Gyimah

Sam Gyimah co-founded and is co-Managing Director of Clearstone Ltd, a company which trains the unemployed and low paid as Heavy Goods Vehicle drivers and places them into jobs. Prior to starting his own business he was an Investment Banker at Goldman Sachs International. Sam is involved with a number of charities; he sits on the boards of Nacro Community Enterprises; was on the board of an inner London School for three years; and is on the Development Board of Somerville College, Oxford. He is Research Secretary of the Bow Group and a Ward Vice Chairman of the Hampstead and Highgate Conservative Association. He graduated from Somerville College, Oxford in 1999 with a degree in Philosophy, Politics and Economics and was President of the Oxford Union.